IMPLEMENTATION OF NATIONAL RURAL EMPLOYMENT GUARANTEE SCHEME :

A CASE STUDY OF UTTAR PRADESH

Implementation of National Rural Employment Guarantee Scheme

A Case Study of Uttar Pradesh

Roshan Lal Raina
G.L. Sharma
S.K. Bajpai

Ess Ess Publications

in association with

Lal Bahadur Shastri Research Centre for Public Policy and Social Change
2008

Published by
Ess Ess Publications
4837/24, Ansari Road,
Darya Ganj,
New Delhi-110 002.
Tel.: 23260807, 41563444
Fax: 41563334
E-mail: info@essessreference.com
www.essessreference.com

In Association with
Lal Bahadur Shastri Research Centre for Public Policy and Social Change
Established in collaboration with Lal Bahadur Shastri Institute of Management, Delhi
1, Moti Lal Nehru Place
New Delhi-110 011
Tel: 011-23018195, 26191081
www.lbsim.ac.in

Rs.425/-

First Published - 2008

ISBN: 81-7000-528-0 (10 Digit)
978-81-7000-528-5 (13 Digit)

Printed at Salasar Imaging Systems

PRINTED IN INDIA

Lal Bahadur Shastri - Man of the Masses

"India is at present engaged in the biggest war of her history — the war against poverty and unemployment"

— **Lal Bahadur Shastri**

New Delhi

May 29, 1956

Foreword

The National Rural Employment Guarantee Scheme (NREGS) is possibly the most ambitious income security programme for India's rural poor in post Independent India. Around 30 per cent of Indians live in absolute poverty and if one were to consider a somewhat wider definition of vulnerability then the percentage moves up to as much as about 77 per cent. Most of the vulnerable are from among the scheduled castes and tribes, the minorities and other backward classes. They also happen to have very low or negligible land holdings and hardly any other assets to speak of other than their labour power. The rural poor principally comprise of landless labourers, who are not even assured of finding work on a daily basis. It is in this context that the NREGS assumes importance since it guarantees 100 days of work to anyone desirous of it at the minimum wage.

The purpose of the scheme is to employ labour to create rural assets. The panchayats and gram sabhas have a very important role to play in this endeavour. Despite the many voices of scepticism that have emanated from establishment economists, the scheme already appears to have found wide support among the rural poor across the length and breadth of the country. There is no denying that there are entrenched interests that are always prone to introduce elements of corruption in the scheme to serve their narrow self interest but that ought not to lead us to question the usefulness of the scheme itself. Armed with the *Right to Information Act,* the rural work force along with panchayats and NGO workers need to unitedly work towards correcting and amending the problems that are being faced rather than think of reneging on the entire project.

Social science research institutions can play a very important role in trying to dispassionately evaluate the working of this scheme and suggest policy measures to enhance its effectiveness. Lal Bahadur Shastri Research Centre for Public Policy and Social Change (LBSRC), *Centre of Excellence* of The Lal Bahadur Shastri Institute of Management, Delhi, must be commended for being in the forefront of doing precisely this. The core team of researchers led by Dr. R L Raina, Dr G.L. Sharma, and Dr S.K. Bajpai have made a very good beginning by conducting a pilot study in four select districts of Uttar Pradesh. They arrive at very interesting findings. Almost 97.25 per cent of the respondents opined that they welcome the implementation of the scheme. In the districts under review, viz., Sitapur, Raebareli, Unnao and Barabanki, there were no women members in the worksites. It would be necessary to explore why this is so and in particular if there are any sociological compulsions that prevent women in these districts from joining the workforce. Among other findings, it is seen that the disabled and the old are also found working under the scheme.

As the Union Government gets set to expand the NREGS to all districts in the country on April 1, 2008, there is great need to have the results of early evaluations of the scheme to reach as wide an audience as is possible.

Pulin B. Nayak
Director, Delhi School of Economics
University of Delhi, Delhi

Preface

Although the Indian economy has achieved a substantial growth rate of 9 percent, the problem of unemployment and poverty in the rural areas of the country continues to be a cause of serious concern. During the last three decades, the rich have become richer and the poor miserably poorer. Even the marginal farmers have become landless labourers. Due to ineffective delivery system and mismanagement of several employment programs initiated by the Central Government, the poor have not been benefited from them. To provide means of livelihood and reduce the quantum of poverty especially in rural areas, the ruling United Progressive Alliance Government at the Centre enacted a law to enable the poor people in the rural areas to get 100 days employment with legal guarantee. This pro- active became a law when the National Rural Employment Guarantee Bill was unanimously passed by the Parliament on August 23, 2005 and notified in September, 2005.

In Uttar Pradesh the most populous state in the country, 39 per cent of its rural population lives below the poverty line. Out of 330 identified backward districts in the country, 39 are in Uttar Pradesh, constituting about 12% of the total backward districts in the country. Out of 22 districts identified in the first phase of NREGA in UP, 4 were selected for the study. Two blocks in each district and two villages in each block were selected for an in-depth study of the impact of NREGA. In all, 400 beneficiaries were interviewed on the worksite in 16 villages through a structured questionnaire meant for the purpose.

It is interesting to note that 61 per cent of the beneficiaries were from Scheduled Caste (SCs) and 37 per cent Other Backward Class (OBCs) benefited from NREGS work. Handicapped persons were also provided job at the work site. Beneficiaries, while expressing satisfaction on the new initiatives taken by the Government, demanded increase in wage rates, and work site facilities as enshrined in the Act and increasing the number of working days in a financial year. However, women were found conspicuously absent at the work site served. There is need for vigorous identification of job opportunity well in advance and strict monitoring of the implementation process. Creating greater awareness about the scheme through various local media facilities available at the rural areas as well as vigorous efforts to involve women workers is also warranted.

NREGA is a strong measure to realize the right to work. This is enshrined in the Constitution of India as one of the Directive Principles. It states, "The state shall in particular direct its policy towards securing — that the citizens, men and women equally have the right to an adequate means of livelihood." The National Rural Employment Guarantee Act aims to tackle the problems of hunger and deprivation, so that the poor households in the rural areas of the country might be saved from destitution.

The Act was initially introduced in the 200 most backward districts on Feb. 2, 2006. With a view to cover entire country, it was extended to another 130 districts from April 1, 2007 and now the government has decided to bring 265 more such districts in the ambit of NREGA from April 1, 2008.

National Rural Employment Guarantee Scheme is in fact A Ray of Hope – for the rural poor and unskilled labourers who have will to work and are looking for opportunities to come out of the clutches of poverty, deprivation and discrimination particularly on economic and social fronts. The need of the hour to implement the national rural employment guarantee scheme in letter and spread. Moreover, there is a need to ensure peoples confidence as the Act described as Peoples Act by implementing the scheme with transparency, vigilance, people's participation and public accountability all through from Center to Gram Panchayat.

The study reveals that there is wide appreciation of the NREGA in the rural areas where as 61 per cent and 37 per cent of the beneficiaries were from Scheduled Castes and Other Backward Classes, but negligible participation from of women and lacks many other amenities at worksites. However, NREGA is a 'Hope for the Poor'.

R.L. Raina

G.L. Sharma

S.K. Bajpai

Acknowledgement

This study was carried out in the state of Uttar Pradesh. Four districts, eight blocks and sixteen villages were selected for the purpose. A total of 400 beneficiaries from sixteen villages were contacted at worksites in various villages of the selected districts. During the study, many government officials like the Chief Development Officer, Project Directors, District Rural Development Agencies, Members of Panchayati Raj Institutions, Block Level Officers, and other functionaries were also contacted and all of them provided valuable information relating to the project. It is very difficult to acknowledge their contribution individually. However, we express our sincere gratitude to all of them for their active involvement and cooperation in the project. The study would not have been possible without ready cooperation of as many as 400 beneficiaries of the National Rural Employment Guarantee Scheme working at their sites in all the 16 villages, spread over the selected districts in Uttar Pradesh, viz., Barabanki, Raebareli, Sitapur and Unnao. These workers actively responded to our structured questionnaire and spoke frankly. We take this opportunity to thank them all.

We acknowledge, with gratitude, the guidance we received from Professor Pulin B. Nayak, during the course of the research work. We specially thank him for his foreword to the book.

We are immensely grateful to Shri Anil Shastri, Chairman, Board of Governors, Lal Bahadur Shastri

Institute of Management, Delhi for encouraging us to undertake the present research work and also for granting required financial assistance.

We would also like to thank Dr. S.P. Pandey, Director, G. B. Pant Institute of Studies in Rural Development, Lucknow for providing assistance in conducting the field survey.

We would like to record our appreciation for Mr. S. Venkatesan, Research Associate at the Lal Bahadur Shastri Research Centre for Public Policy and Social Change, New Delhi for his assiduous assistance and suggestions towards preparation of this research report. Dr. Sangeeta Chhabra, Professor, LBSIM, Delhi deserves special thanks for her expert advice in some of the key areas. Mr. Naresh Wadhwa, LBSIM, Delhi deserves our thanks for extending his support in tedious data entry. We also wish to place on record a word of appreciation for M/s. Ess Ess Publications, New Delhi for organizing the publication of this book in a record time.

Contents

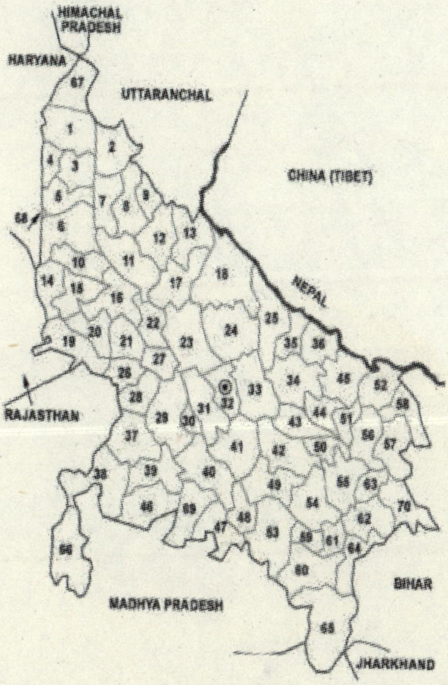

1. Muzaffarnagar
2. Bijnor
3. Meerut
4. Baghpat
5. Ghaziabad
6. Bulandshahr
7. Jyotiba Phule Nagar
8. Moradabad
9. Rampur
10. Aligarh
11. Budaun
12. Barielly
13. Pilibhit
14. Mathura
15. Hathras
16. Etah
17. Shahjahanpur
18. Lakhimpur
19. Agra
20. Firozabad
21. Mainpuri
22. Farrukhabad
23. Hardoi
24. Sitapur
25. Bharaich
26. Etawah
27. Kannauj
28. Aurlayan
29. Kanpur (Rural)
30. Kanpur (Urban)
31. Unnao
32. Lucknow
33. Barabanki
34. Gonda
35. Shravasti
36. Balrampur
37. Jalaun
38. Sonbhadra
39. Hamirpur
40. Fatehpur
41. Rae Barirlly
42. Sultanpur
43. Faizabad
44. Basti
45. Sidharthnagar
46. Mahoba
47. Chitrakut
48. Kaushambi
49. Pratapgarh
50. Ambedkarnagar
51. Sant Kabir Nagar
52. Maharajganj
53. Allahabad
54. Jaunpur
55. Azamgarh
56. Gorakhpur
57. Deoria
58. Kushinagar
59. Sant Ravi Nagar
60. Mirzapur
61. Varanasi
62. Ghazipur
63. Mau
64. Chandauli
65. Sonbhadra
66. Lalitpur
67. Saharanpur
68. Gautam Budh Nagar
69. Banda
70. Ballia

Districts under NREGA

Azamgarh, Banda, Barabanki, Chandauli, Chitrakoot, Fatehpur, Gorakhpur, Hamirpur, Hardoi, Jalaun, Jaunpur, Kaushambi, Kheri, Kushinagar, Lalitpur, Mahoba, Mirzapur, Pratapgarh, Raebareli, Sitapur, Sonebhadra and Unnao (22)

Districts Surveyed

Barabanki, Raebareli, Sitapur and Unnao (4)

About the Authors

R.L. Raina, Ph.D. has over 25 years of academic and managerial experience. He has had several prestigious assignments in Educational institutes in US, UK, France, Germany and Canada. Reputed organizations like the Fulbright Foundation (USA), the British Council (UK), the Max Muller Bhawan (Germany), the ESCP-EAP (France), and the IDRC (Canada) sponsored these assignments. In terms of research, he has authored 2 and edited 9 best selling books, and has made significant contributions (95 research papers in all to date) in several reputed national and international journals: the areas include 'Business Communication, Corporate & Media Relations', TQM', 'IT Applications', 'HRM' and 'Marketing' in the Information Sector'. He has also presented over 110 papers in national and international conferences/seminars floated by reputed organizations, universities included. He has been heavily involved in conducting MDPs and Workshops. Concurrently, he has been involved in consulting and research assignments awarded by organizations like the JSI, Deliver, USA, IDRC, Canada. The Johns Hopkins University/Centre for Communication Programmes, Baltimore, USA, the UP State Electricity Board, Public Affairs section of the US, Department of State and the MHRD (GOI). Dr. Raina is a life member of several professional bodies in the country and holds the unique distinction of having bagged three of the top professional bodies in the country and holds the unique distinction of having bagged three of the top professional honours / awards. Before joining LBSIM, Dr. Raina was Professor, 'Communication' at the Indian Institute of Management, Lucknow (IIML), where he was also responsible for developing and managing state-of-the-art world class academic infrastructure, including the learning resource centre. At IIML, Prof. Raina also successfully initiated and handled activities in areas like 'Corporate Communication', Media Relations' Student Affairs, and 'Alumni Affairs'.

G.L. Sharma, M.Com., Ph. D from University of Rajasthan, has been in teaching and research for over four decades and is a Professor of Finance and Accounting at this Institute. Dr. G.L. Sharma's area of teaching and research are Accounting and Finance. During 1982-1985 he was a Reader in Finance, Department of Business Administration, Ahmedu Bello University, Zaria, Nigeria. He also completed a Research Project on "Institutional Financing of Small Scale Industries in Nigeria and special reference to Northern States (A Comparative Study of Nigeria and India)". He has published 6 books including Advanced Cost Accounting, Cost Analysis & Control – A Managerial Approach and Theory & Techniques of Cost Accounting. He has jointly edited three books – "Corporate Finance: Emerging Options", Contemporary Issues in Business Finance & Taxation" and a book on "Leveraging Human Potential for Excellence". He has contributed large numbers of research articles in leading Journals. Currently, he is working on research project "Activity Based Costing in Indian Industry". Dr. Sharma is the Managing Editor of LBS Journal of Management & Research. He is Secretary General of Indian Financial Management Association and also Managing Editor of Indian Journal of Finance & Research. He has widely travelled both in India and Abroad.

S.K. Bapai, Ph.D. from Lucknow University has been associated in several research and consultancy projects related to corporate as well as social sectors for two decades. He has published research papers and articles in professional journals, newspapers and magazines. He is member of Educational Advisory Board of two professional journals also. He has also provided consultancy as Training Expert under the aegis of Water and Power Consultancy Ltd., a Government of India Undertaking which was responsible for Monitoring and Evaluation of 'UP Sodic Land Reclamation Project – II' (a World Bank assisted project). Presently he is with Lal Bahadur Shastri Research Centre for Public Policy and Social Change, a *'Centre of Excellence'* of Lal Bahadur Shastri Institute of Management, Delhi.

1
Introduction

The Constitution of India refers to the Right to Work under the "Directive Principles of State Policy". Article 39 envisages the state to ensure that citizens, men and women equally have the right to an adequate means to livelihood. Further, Article 41 emphasizes that the state within the limits of its economic capacity and development will make effective provision for securing 'Right to Work'. This was to be achieved through a systematic public intervention in terms of policies and planning popularly known as Five Year Plans. The First Five Year Plan (1951-56) stressed that "A programme for full employment with assurance of minimum wage to the newly employed can get into swing as the capital formation in the community goes up and poverty can disappear" (Government of India, 1953: P. 8)[1].

Though this broad approach has been followed all-through the Five-Year Plans, the direct anti-poverty programmes including employment generation schemes, were started from the Sixth Five Year Plan (1982-87) onwards. In order to provide direct wage employment to the rural poor through public works and to eradicate poverty, several programmes were implemented by the Central as well as the State Governments. The major schemes introduced by the Central Government are: National Rural Employment Programme (NREP) 1980-89; Rural Landless Employment Guarantee Programme (RLEGP) 1983-89;

Jawahar Rozgar Yojana (JRY) 1989-99; Employment Assurance Scheme (EAS) 1993-99; Jawahar Gram Samridhi Yojana (JGSY) 1999-2002; Sampoorna Grameen Rozgar Yojana (SGRY) since September 2001; National Food for Work Programme (NFFWP) since November 14, 2004; Maharashtra Employment Guarantee Scheme (MEGS), which commenced in 1965, continued to be an important state-level wage-employment programme (Economic Survey, 2007)[2].

RATIONALE OF THE NATIONAL RURAL EMPLOYMENT GUARANTEE ACT, 2005

The National Rural Employment Act, 2005 (NREGA) draws on the experience of above mentioned programmes in terms of their impact on the well-being of rural poor as far as poverty reduction and employment generation are concerned. The experiences during the last 50 years or so indicate that there has been some progress at the national level; however, it has also shown wide variations in terms of regional and social contexts. Even today, a majority of rural people especially the socially disadvantaged groups (Scheduled Castes and Tribes) live in absolute poverty and depend mainly on the wages they earn through unskilled, casual and manual labour. They are often on the threshold levels of subsistence without productive employment and remain vulnerable to chronic poverty. Therefore, the National Rural Employment Guarantee Act 2005 (NREGA) has been formulated to provide guarantee of livelihood security in rural areas of the country.

The following account provides the details of poverty and unemployment situation in the country as a whole and particularly in the context of the state of Uttar Pradesh where the present study attempts to examine the performance of the NREGA.

POVERTY SITUATION[i] AND PATTERN OF POVERTY REDUCTION

The pattern of poverty reduction trends reveal three distinct phases. The first phase, from the beginning of planning era in the 1950s to the mid-1970s was characterised by wide variation by year to year with no significant improvement in poverty reduction. During the early period of 1950s, more than half of India's population suffered from abject poverty. The absolute number of poor accounted for about three-fourth of India's poor, rose from 182 million in 1956-67 to 261 million in 1973-74 (Ahluwalia 1978[3], Tendulkar and L.R. Jain 1995[4] and Dandekar 1996[5]).[ii] The decline in poverty level was more pronounced in the second phase of the period during 1980 – 1990. The incident of poverty level was 45 per cent in 1983 which declined to 39 per cent in 1987-88. In the third phase of poverty trend during the nineties and early 2000 (1990-2005), considered to be a post-reform period, the poverty reduction was witnessed with significant regional variation in progress and setbacks (Jha, Raghbendra 2002[6] and Radhakrishna and Shoven Ray, 2005[7]).

In the post reform period, in 1993-94, about 36 per cent of population was living below the poverty

---

i The estimates of poverty , based on a minimum nutritional flows, i.e. 2400 calorie per capita per day in the rural areas and 2100 calorie in the urban areas, for the years, viz. 1973-74, 1977-78, 1983, 1987-88, 1993-94 & 1999-2000 as per official methodology.

ii There are numerous studies on poverty reduction and trends covering relatively for the longer period. For example, a study by Raghbendra Jha (2002) provides the estimates of poverty and its pattern during 1950-51 to 1999-2000. See also Tendulkar S and L.R. Jain, 1995, and Radhakrishna, R and Shoven Ray, 2005.

line but it declined to 26 per cent in 1999-2000. The most recent estimates of poverty for the year 2004-05 show that the proportion of population living below poverty line was 22.7 percent based on 365 days recall period and 28.5 percent based on 30 days recall period[iii] (Sen and Himanshu 2004[8]). Irrespective of the proportion that was estimated to be poor in India over the years, the estimate of absolute number of poor continues to remain around 320 million, according to 30-day recall period method (Sen, Abhijit 1996[9] and Planning Commission 2002[10]).

The poverty has declined faster in all states during the 1990s than the early 1970s, though the size and pace of reduction varied. Only five states, viz. Andhra Pradesh, Gujarat, Haryana, Kerala and Punjab were able to reduce poverty by more than 50 per cent. Between 1987 and 1994, the incidence of poverty increased in Assam, Bihar and Uttar Pradesh. As a result, the regional concentration of poverty got accentuated in major three states, viz. Bihar, Madhya Pradesh, and Uttar Pradesh, where half of India's rural population lives in poverty. (Datt and Ravallion 1998[11], Ahluwalia 2000[12], World Bank 2002[13] and Economic Survey 2007[14]).

UNEMPLOYMENT SITUATION AND PATTERN OF EMPLOYMENT GROWTH

The issue of 'employment for all' has been one of the policy concerns ever since the beginning of planning in India. The performance can be best captured by

iii Comparison of poverty reduction during the post reform period is debatable mainly due to the methodological changes in the NSS data collection. Several scholars have debated on this, for instance See Sen and Himanshu (2004) for detailed discussion.

the rate of growth in employment or fall in unemployment rate. The major source of information for examining the pattern and trend of employment and unemployment is the National Sample Surveys periodically conducted by the National Sample Survey Organization (NSSO). The NSSO has conducted seven quintessential surveys for the periods 1972-73 to 2004-05, which provide three different measures of employment and unemployment, viz. Usual Principle Status (UPS), Current Weekly Status (CWS) and Current Daily Status (CDS). For each category, person employed, unemployed, out of labour force were recorded during these surveys[iv].

According to the NSS Survey for the period of 1970s, the employment rate was 42 percent but it was higher for men at 54.3 per cent and lower for women at 29.7 per cent in 1977-78 (NSSO Reports[15] and Planning Commission 2001[16]). There was no significant change in employment rate after this period and it almost remained at 42 per cent in 2004-05. Similarly the unemployment rate varied between 2 per cent and 2.8 per cent for men and women respectively in rural areas. As we move from the usual status to the weekly or daily status, the unemployment rate appears to rise substantially. During 1993-94, it was 6% in the rural sector among men and women on a daily-status basis, indicating large seasonal or intermittent unemployment in India (Sen 1996[17], Sundaram K 2001[18] and Government of India, NSSO Reports[19]).

---

iv Usual Principle Status (UPS), that indicates a status in terms of major time over the 365 days; Current Weekly Status (CWS) where the reference period is the week i.e. the 7 days preceding the interview and Current Daily Status (CDS) that reflects labour time disposition during each day of the week in terms of two half days

The recent NSS survey (61st Round) for the period July 2004 – June 2005 indicates that the changes in employment and unemployment scenario during last decade has been sluggish on the whole. It may be mentioned that more than 47 million persons were provided employment between 2000 and 2005. Further, the survey reveals that during 1999-2000 to 2004-05, the labour force increased even faster at an annual 2.54 per cent as compared to annual employment growth of 2.48 per cent. Therefore, unemployment on basis of UPS was higher, i.e. 3.06 per cent in 2004-05 as compared to 2.78 per cent during 1999-00. The incidence of unemployment rate based on Current Daily Status (CDS) increased over the period from 6 per cent during 1972-73 to 8 per cent during 2004-05 (Sharma, Shailendra 2004[20] and NSSO Reports[21]).

POVERTY AND UNEMPLOYMENT SITUATION IN UTTAR PRADESH

The foregoing data description at the national level show the wide variation in the poverty reduction and employment growth in India. However, it does not reveal regional or state variation in the progress. Therefore, the following paragraphs focus on poverty and unemployment situation in the state of Uttar Pradesh with an all-India comparison.

The incidence of poverty and reduction in poverty level in the state of Uttar Pradesh and all-India is depicted in the Figure 1.1. It is clear that during the span of 26 years, i.e. from 1973-99, the poverty level decreased from about 57% in 1973-74 to 31% in 1999-2000. This indicates a reduction of about 26 percentage points during the above mentioned period. It is also noticed from the figure that reduction in the incidence of poverty has mainly taken place from 1993-94 to 1999-2000. An almost similar trend is observed in poverty reduction at an all-India level. However, the pace of reduction is more prominent at the national level as the percentage of population living below the poverty line declined from 54.88% in 1973-74 to 26.10% in 1999-2000 (about 29 percentage points), while corresponding reduction at the state level was from 57.07% to 31.15%, i.e. about 26 percentage points (Government of Uttar Pradesh[22]). This is indicative of deterioration in U.P.'s relative poverty position over the years. Uttar Pradesh is the only state among 14 major states of the country which had substantial proportion of the total poor population in the country (See Annexure 1).

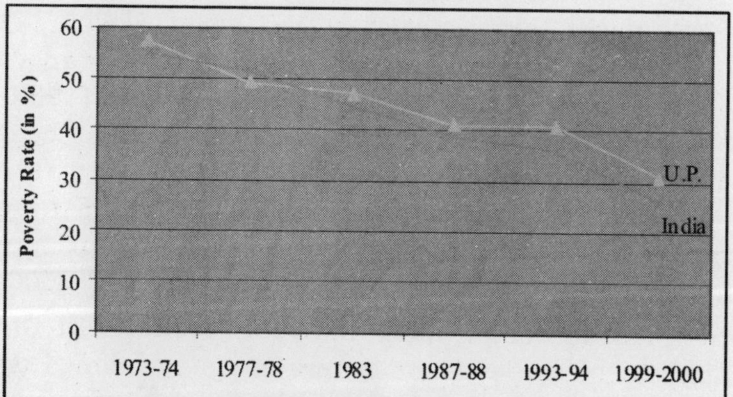

Fig. 1.1. Poverty Trend in Uttar Pradesh (1973-74 to 1999-2000)

Source: Human Development Report 2003: Uttar Pradesh

Regarding the unemployment trends, the employment and unemployment survey conducted by the National Sample Survey Organisation for the period1973-74 to 1999-2000 as depicted in Figure 1.2

is more revealing. It indicates an increasing trend of unemployment rate from 3.75 per cent in 1973-74 to 4.33 per cent in 1983.

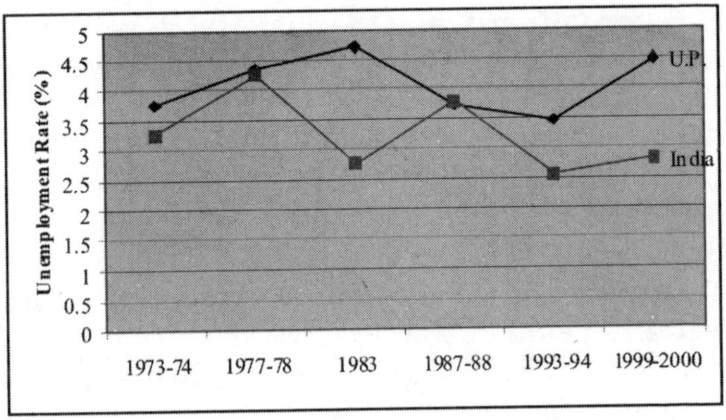

Fig. 1.2 Trends in Unemployment in Uttar Pradesh (1973-74 to 1999-2000)

Source: Human Development Report 2003: Uttar Pradesh

However, the unemployment rate began to decline significantly during the late 1980s (1987-88). It decreased from 4.71 per cent to 3.73 per cent during 1983-88. Further, unemployment rate declined but in a slower pace up to 1993-94. During the post-reform periodm, the unemployment rate increased to the level of 4.48 per cent in 1999-2000.

The foregoing data analysis reveals that the impacts of employment generation programmes on poverty alleviation has not been as expected. The rate of improvement in employment growth has not been enough to absorb the growth of labor force which resulted in a significant proportion of the population left unemployed. This is a particularly common phenomenon that the impact has not significantly helped poverty reduction and employment growth in the poorer states such as Uttar Pradesh..

The unsatisfactory performance of the earlier employment schemes has been due to certain lacunae in the process of their implementation. In fact, the wage employment programmes could generate only relief-type employment opportunities rather than creating productive assets. Without this, public works programmes cannot contribute in the generation of sustainable and productive employment (Hirway and Terhal, 1997[23]; Dev, 2004[24]). Further there was also criticism of lack of awareness, lack of community participation, lack of planning, diversion of funds, lack of monitoring and verification system and lack of public accountability.

MAHARASHTRA EMPLOYMENT GUARANTEE SCHEME: EXPERIENCE

The Employment Guarantee Scheme in Maharashtra is the longest ever surviving programme of its kind. It is unique because of its design and execution shows clarity of goals as well as consistency in approach. (Bagchi, 2005[25]). The scheme grew out of the pilot experiment carried out in Sangli, Maharashtra in 1965, known as the Page Scheme named after V.S. Page. Later in 1970, the same was extended to cover eleven districts and subsequently in the 1972, to the entire state.

The employment was guaranteed to all able bodied adults who asked for it. This was implemented by the existing administrative system in the state at very little additional cost. The important feature of the scheme was the largest state sponsored public works program focused on the alleviation of poverty, and guaranteed gainful employment to all adults above 18 years of age in rural areas and 'C' class Municipal Councils. Selection for employment was based on the willingness to undertake unskilled manual work on a piece rate basis and self-targeting. The important short-term objective listed was to add to household income based on employment and to contribute to the development of rural infrastructure and create sustained employment opportunities in the long run. There were provisions like unemployment allowance, provision of shelter and first aid, and no discrimination on the basis of gender or caste. The Employment Guarantee Schemes (EGS) benefited the people in several ways as it provided employment and income earning opportunities, food security for the poor, income stability and equality of wages offered to men and women (Krishnaraj, et al, 2003[26]).

Some of the flaws that were identified in the implementation process of the Maharashtra Employment Guarantee Scheme may be mentioned as — gap between commencement of work and payment; non-availability of continuous employment; leakage due to under-utilization of the funds; no unemployment allowance; low awareness of entitlements among the workers; absence of linkages between works and larger plans for the district; skill upgradation provided under the Act was not enough, so dependence on EGS for employment, subjective calculation of wages, the muster role of a particular site was almost impossible to trace after the period of 15 days required for the payment of wages, work was done by a group of both men and women, so calculation of the individual share of wages, especially of women was somewhat subjective and depended on the team leader who was usually male, as well as other co-workers; expected benefits in the form of equalization of wages and increased access to income did not materialize; maternity benefits did not reach women as eligibility for this benefits requires proving 75 days of work, and changing work sites and inadequate records made it difficult for women to show the stipulated days of work; shelter and crèches were not provided as work sites were temporary; no toilets were found near/ on the EGS sites; under-utilization of available funds, etc. (Krishnraj, et al, 2003[27])

In this context, there are some of the challenges before such employment guarantee scheme. These may include:

— lack of local participation (poorest people often continue to work for contractors even when public works are going on).
— Over dependence on bureaucracy
— Rigidity of schemes
— Pilferage of resources, leakages and corruption;
— Supply–driven wage – employment schemes;
— Inadequate employment generation;
— Inability to provide minimum livelihood security;
— Cheating and delay in wage payment;
— Lack of amenities to workers;
— Poor participation of women;
— Employment opportunities inflexible to workers' demand;
— Lack of transparency in employment and cash disbursement;
— Fudging of muster rolls;
— Employment of children;
— Lack of proper communication of the scheme;

Despite the above stated shortcomings in implementation, the significance of the EGS lies in its impact on the overall development process and in inviting the participation of poor people as well.

THE CONTEXT OF NREG ACT, 2005

The National Rural Employment Guarantee Act, 2005 has emerged as an important legislative measure to address poverty and unemployment. This Act ensures the livelihood security for people in rural areas by guaranteeing 100 days of employment in a financial year to a rural household. The Government of India passed the "National Rural Employment Guarantee Act 2005" (NREGA 2005) towards partial fulfillment of a constitutional obligations under Article 41 of the Indian Constitution that provides 'Right to Work' to the citizens of the country. The Act received assent of the President on September 5, 2005 and was notified in the Gazette of India on September 7, 2005 (Government of India, 2006)[28].

SALIENT FEATURE OF NATIONAL RURAL EMPLOYMENT GUARANTEE ACT, 2005

This legislation is unique and makes a path-breaking shift in its implementation vis-à-vis existing other wage employment programmes because it gives legal-constitutional guarantee to ensure minimum of 100 days wage employment to every rural household whose adult members are willing to do unskilled manual work at the prevailing minimum wages (Government of India 2006[29]).

In fact, the Act also highlights the legislative role of Panchayats in complying their fundamental duty as stated in the 73rd constitutional amendment of providing "Economic Development and Social Justice" in the rural areas. The acknowledgement of Panchayati Raj Institutions (PRIs) as the Principal Agencies for the implementation under this Act has unleashed enormous opportunities for decentralized development. It encourages local solutions to local livelihood challenges.

The present study, therefore, attempts to understand the NREGA implementation process, progress in the selected districts of Uttar Pradesh and also tries to provide suggestions and recommendations for its effective implementation.

OBJECTIVES

The present study makes a modest attempt to probe whether:

— there is a general awareness about the scheme among the poor rural workers;

— the scheme is providing jobs to the eligible applicants without hassles;

— the beneficiaries and villagers appreciate the implementation of the scheme;

— the projects undertaken in the villages have potential to create job opportunities in the area, and;

— finally, to make suggestions for making the scheme more beneficial to the rural people living below the poverty line.

RESEARCH METHODOLOGY

The principal thrust of the survey of the beneficiaries at the worksites in different villages is to understand their perspective about the NREG Act, its implementation mechanism and impact. In order to make an in-depth study, the state of Uttar Pradesh

(U.P) has been selected for the present survey. The Government of U.P. by a notification from Rural Development Section – 7, No. 107/38-7-2006-8 NREGA dated February 8, 2007 has formulated UP Rural Employment Guarantee Scheme as required by the NREGA, 2005 and the scheme has been implemented in 22 poorest districts. These are Azamgarh, Banda, Barabanki, Chandauli, Chitrakoot, Fatehpur, Gorakhpur, Hamirpur, Hardoi, Jalaum, Jaunpur, Kaushambi, Kheri, Kushinagar, Lalitpur, Mahoba, Mirzapur, Pratapgarh, Raebareli, Sitapuri, Sonebhadra and Unnao. These identified districts in Uttar Pradesh account for 11 per cent of total 200 most backward districts identified in the first phase of NREGA implementation.

This study is based on both the secondary and the primary data. The secondary data have been collected from various sources published by the Government as well as from the official NREGA website. The collection of primary data has been accomplished by administering a structured questionnaire on the beneficiaries employed at the work sites in the sixteen villages of selected four districts, viz. Barabanki, Raebarely, Sitapur and Unnao during Dec. 2006 – Feb 2007.

The districts have been selected on convenient sampling basis. The selection of two blocks from each district and two villages from each block has been made randomly. The number of beneficiaries interviewed at each worksite was 25. Thus, 100 beneficiaries from each district were interviewed, making the total sample size of 400 beneficiaries. (For the list of selected blocks, villages in each district and the structured questionnaire, see Annexure 2 and 3).

In order to administer the interview schedule of the beneficiaries, we identified well qualified and trained investigators from a reputed research organization, Pandit G.B. Pant Institute of studies in Rural Development in Lucknow. It may be judicious to mention that this Institute, in its eighteen years of existence has completed more than 60 research studies sponsored by Central and State Government ministries besides the Planning Commission, New Delhi.

LIMITATION AND SCOPE

The study has several limitations as number of selected districts, blocks, villages and beneficiaries are small. Therefore, there is still a great scope for conducting in-depth survey in each district at various levels besides the workers at sites in the villages. The probing into the aspect of social audit of the works undertaken would certainly provide useful insights into the process of implementation of NREGA and its effectiveness. Along with this, survey of registered households, job cards holders and other villagers besides throwing light on the financial management of NREGA would also be immensely rewarding.

CHAPTER SCHEME

The foregone description forms the subject matter of Chapter One, which includes the rationale of the study, objectives, research methodology and focus of the present study. Chapter Two describes the National Rural Employment Guarantee Act, 2005 and mechanism of NREGA implementation. The subject matter has been heavily drawn from the Operational Guidelines published by the Ministry of Rural Development, Government of India in this Chapter. Chapter Three describes the study area, i.e. the brief profile of Uttar Pradesh, the selected districts, viz.

Barabanki, Raebareli, Sitapur and Unnao; the available relevant data about the selected villages, and methodology of survey. Chapter Four presents macro level analysis of NREGS performance in the state of U.P. at district levels based on secondary data. Chapter Five presents the analysis of responses from the beneficiaries working at various worksites in the selected villages according to the filled-in structured questionnaires and lastly, Chapter Six summarises the major findings and suggestions.

REFERENCES

1 Government of India, First Five Year Plan: Planning Commission, New Delhi 1953

2 Economic Survey, 2006-07, Ministry of Finance, Economic Division, Government of India, 2007

3 Ahluwalia, Montek S (1978): 'Rural Poverty and Agricultural Performance in India', *Journal of Development Studies,* 14(3): 298-323.

4 Tendulkar, S.D. and L.R Jain (1995) "Economic reforms and poverty" *Economic and Political Weekly,* Bombay: June 10

5 Dandekar, V. M. (1996) *The Indian Economy: 1947-92,* Vol. 2: *Population, Poverty and Employment,* Sage Publications, New Delhi.

6 Jha, Raghbendra (2002), Reducing Poverty and Inequality in India: Has Liberalization Helped?, *Economic and Political Weekly,* June.

7 Radhakrishna, R and Shoven Ray (eds.), Handbook of Poverty in India: Perspective, Policies and Programs; Oxford University Press, New Delhi, 2005

8 Sen, Abhijit and Himanshu (2004), 'Poverty and Inequality in India, *Economic and Political Weekly,* Special Article, February

9 Sen, Abhijit (1996), "Economic Reforms, Employment and Poverty: Trends and Options", *Economic and Political Weekly,* September

10 Planning Commission (2002): '*National Human Development*

Report-2001, Govt. of India, New Delhi,

11 Datt, G. and M. Ravallion (1998) Why have some Indian states done better than others at reducing rural poverty?, *Economica,* 65 (1), pp. 17-38.

12 Ahluwalia, M. S., (2000), 'Economic Performance of States in Post-Reforms Period', *Economic and Political Weekly,* May.

13 World Bank (2002), 'Poverty In India: The Challenge of Uttar Pradesh' (Draft). PREM: South Asia Region

14 Economic Survey (2006-07), Ministry of Finance, Economic Division, Government of India, New Delhi, 2007.

15 National Sample Survey Organization (NSSO), Report on Employment and Unemployment Situation in India, (Reports for various rounds for the period 19973-74 to 2004-05), Ministry of Statistics and Programme Implementation, New Delhi.

16 Planning Commission (2001): *'Report of Task Force on Employment Opportunities',* New Delhi, June.

17 Sen, Abhijit (1996), "Economic Reforms, Employment and Poverty: Trends and Options" *Economic and Political Weekly,* September

18 Sundaram, K. (2001): 'Employment-Unemployment Situation in Nineties: Some Results from NSS 55th Round Survey', *Economic & Political Weekly,* March 17.

19 National Sample Survey Organization (NSSO), Report on Employment and Unemployment Situation in India, (Rports for various rounds for the period 19973-74 to 2004-05), Ministry of Statistics and Programme Implementation, New Delhi.

20 Sharma, Shailendra (2004): 'Employment in India: Vision 2020', p-221, *'The Report of the S.P Gupta Committee on India Vision 2020',* Planning Commission, New Delhi.

21 National Sample Survey Organization (NSSO), Report on Employment and Unemployment Situation in India, (Reports for various rounds for the period 19973-74 to 2004-05), Ministry of Statistics and Programme Implementation, New Delhi.

22 Government of Utter Pradesh (2007), Human Development Report 2003: Uttar Pradesh, State Planning Commission, U.P. Yojana Bhawan, Lucknow.

23 Hirway, I And P. Terhal (1997), Towards Employment Guarantee in India; Indian and International Experiences in Public Works Programme, Sage Publications: New Delhi.

24 Dev, Mahendra, S. (2004), "Safety Nets for the Chronic Poor in India : An Overview" in A.K. Mehta and A. Shepherd (eds) Chronic Poverty and Development Policy in India, Sage Publications, New Delhi.

25 Bagchee, A. (2005), Political and Administrative Realties of Employment Guarantee Scheme, *Economic and Political Weekly*, October 15, pp 4531- 3537

26 Krishnraj M., et. al. (2003), Gender Sensitive Analysis of Employment Guarantee Scheme, UNIFEM, Delhi.

27 ——(2003), Gender Sensitive Analysis of Employment Guarantee Scheme, UNIFEM, Delhi.

28 Government of India, Ministry of Rural Development, National Rural Employment Guarantee Act, 2005 (NREGA), New Delhi, 2006.

29 Government of India, Ministry of Rural Development, National Rural Employment Guarantee Act, 2005 (NREGA), New Delhi, 2006.

2

National Rural Employment Guarantee Act, 2005

The provision of gainful 'employment for all' was one of the policy goals of India. Since the First Five-year Plan, there have been, accordingly, many programme interventions in this regard. Although there has been an improvement in employment generation through these programmes in rural areas over the years, some sections of rural population especially those unskilled, casual, manual labourers remained unaffected by these measures. This was mainly because these programmes typically offered by the government on the basis of some programme launched by the central and/or state governments. There was no guarantee for job security or payment of the wages which compelled the government to provide guaranteed jobs and wages. However, at the State level, the Government of Maharashtra formulated the Maharashtra Employment Guarantee Scheme under the Maharashtra Employment Guarantee Act, 1977 to provide wage-employment to those who demanded it and thereby, giving a statutory framework to wage employment programmes.

THE NATIONAL RURAL EMPLOYMENT GUARANTEE ACT, 2005

Based on the experience of these programmes,

the National Rural Employment Guarantee Act (NREGA) was enacted to reinforce the commitment towards livelihood security in rural areas. The Act was notified on 7th September, 2005 (The Gazette of India[1]). The significance of NREGA lies in the fact that it creates a right-based framework for wage employment programmes and makes the Government legally accountable for providing employment to those who ask for it. This Chapter describes the basic objective, salient features and the key implementation mechanism of NREGA.

OBJECTIVE OF THE ACT

The basic objective of the Act is to enhance livelihood security in rural areas by providing at least 100 days of guaranteed wage employment in a financial year to every household whose adult members volunteer to do unskilled manual work. The Act initially came into force in 200 districts with effect from 2nd February 2006. The Act has also intent to serve other objectives such as generating productive assets, protecting the environment, empowering rural women, reducing rural-urban migration and fostering social equity[2].

IMPLEMENTATION MECHANISM

Chart 2.1 displays mechanism of implementation and key bodies and functionaries that are responsible for the effective implementation of the Act. According to the NREGA Operational Guidelines, the Ministry of Rural Development, Government of India is the nodal Ministry for the implementation of NREGA. It is required to set up the Central Council which will be responsible for ensuring timely and adequate resource support to the states.

It will undertake regular review, monitoring

and evaluation of processes and outcomes. It will establish a Management Information System (MIS) to capture and track data on every critical aspect of implementation, and assess the utilization of resources through a set of performance indicators. It will support innovations that help in improving processes towards the achievement of the objectives of the Act. It will support the use of Information Technology (IT) to increase the efficiency and transparency of the processes as well as improve interface with the public. It will also ensure that the implementation of NREGA at all levels is sought to be made transparent and accountable to the public.

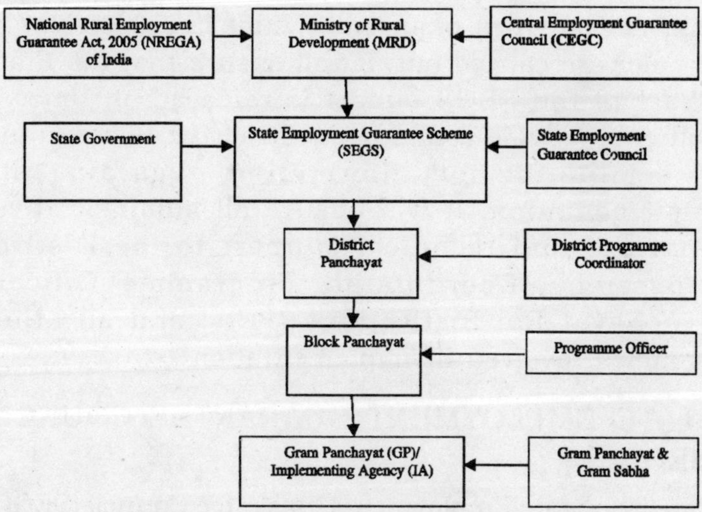

Chart 2.1. Implementation Mechanism

CENTRAL EMPLOYMENT GUARANTEE COUNCIL (CEGC)

The NREGA operational guidelines indicate that the Central Employment Guarantee Council (CEGC) will be responsible for advising the Central Government on NREGA-related matters, and for monitoring and evaluating the implementation of the Act. It shall prepare Annual Reports on the implementation of NREGA and submit these to the Parliament[3].

THE STATE GOVERNMENT

As per the NREG Act, 2005, the State Government has to formulate a Rural Employment Guarantee Scheme (REGS), and the Rules relevant to its implementation, under Section 4 of the Act. It will set up the SEGC (State Employment Guarantee Council) as stated under Section 12 and also designate an officer as the State Rural Employment Guarantee Commissioner responsible for ensuring that all activities required to fulfil the objectives of the Act are carried out. It will ensure that the State Share of the REGS budget is released on time. It will ensure wide communication of the Scheme and dissemination of information regarding its implementation. It will ensure all administrative, financial and technical support to the District Programme Coordinator, Programme Officer, Panchayat Raj Institutions (PRIs) and all other agencies involved in implementation[4].

STATE EMPLOYMENT GUARANTEE COUNCIL (SEGC)

The State Employment Guarantee Council (SEGC) is required to advise the State Government on the implementation of the Scheme, and evaluate and monitor it. It will also decide on the 'preferred works' to be implemented under REGS, and prepare Annual Reports for submission to the State Legislature[5].

DISTRICT PANCHAYAT

Further the operational guidelines state that the

District Panchayat will be responsible for finalizing the District Plans and for monitoring and supervising the REGS in the District[6]. It can also execute works from among the 50 per cent that are not to be implemented by the Gram Panchayats. The State Government will designate a District Programme Co-ordinator (DPC), who shall be responsible for the overall coordination and implementation of the scheme in the District.

BLOCK LEVEL PANCHAYAT

The Block Panchayat will be responsible for planning at the Block level, and for monitoring and supervision. It can also be given the responsibility of executing works from among the 50 *per cent* that are not to be executed by the Gram Panchayat. A full-time officer will be appointed as the Programme Officer at the Block level, who shall be responsible for coordinating the works undertaken by the Gram Panchayat and the implementing agencies at the Block level[7].

GRAM SABHA

The Gram Panchayat has a pivotal role in the implementation of REGS as per the NREGA operational guidelines. It is responsible for planning of works, registering households, issuing job cards, allocating employment, executing 50 per cent of the works, and monitoring the implementation of the Scheme at the village level. The Gram Sabha should also facilitate the implementation of the Scheme, by acting as a forum for sharing information about the Scheme, and also in ensuring transparency and accountability[8].

Apart from Panchayats, Line Departments, NGOs, Central and State Government Undertakings, and Self-Help Groups (SHGs) can also be identified as

Implementing Agencies.

MAJOR FEATURES OF THE ACT

The major features of Act related to work guarantee, implementation process and accountability are as follows:

— Adult members of a rural household may apply for employment if they are willing to do unskilled manual work.

— Such a household will have to apply for registration to the local Gram Panchayat in writing or orally.

— The Gram Panchayat, after due verification, will issue a Job Card to the household as a whole. The Job Card will bear the photograph of all adult members of the household willing to work under NREGA. The Job Card with photograph is free of cost.

— A Job Card-holding household may submit a written application for employment to the Gram Panchayat, stating the time and duration when work is sought. The minimum days of employment have to be fifteen days.

— The Gram Panchayat will issue a dated receipt of the written application for employment, against which the fifteen-day guarantee to provide employment operates.

— Employment will be given within 15 days of application for work by an employment seeker.

— If employment is not provided within 15 days, *daily unemployment allowance in cash* has to be paid. Liability of payment of Unemployment Allowance is *on the States.*

— At least one-third of persons to whom work is allotted have to be women.

— Wages are to be paid according to minimum wages as prescribed under the Minimum Wages Act 1948 for agricultural labourers in the state, unless the Centre notifies a wage rate which will not be less than Rs 60 per day.

— Disbursement of wages has to be done on a weekly basis and not beyond a fortnight.

— Panchayat Raj Institutions [PRIs] have a principal role in planning and implementation.

— Each district has to prepare a shelf of "Projects." The instrument for providing employment are to be works selected from the list of permissible works.

— Work should ordinarily be provided within a 5 km radius of the village or else extra wages of 10% are payable.

— Work-site facilities such as crèche, drinking water, shade have to be provided.

— Social Audit has to be done by the Gram Sabha.

— Grievance redressal mechanisms have to be put in place for ensuring a responsive implementation process.

— All accounts and records relating to the Scheme are to be made available to any person desirous of obtaining a copy of such records on demand and after paying a specified fee.

FUNDING PATTERN

The Government of India (GoI) has established a fund called the National Employment Guarantee Fund[9], from which grants are released directly to Districts. Revolving funds are to be set up under REGS at the

District, Block and Gram Panchayat levels, with separate bank accounts being opened for such funds at each level.

Each Rural Employment Guarantee Scheme is required to have the minimum features specified in Schedule I and Schedule II of the Act. Section 4 of the Act also provides that until such a Scheme is notified by the State Government, the Annual or Perspective Plan of the Sampoorna Grameen Rozgar Yojana (SGRY) or the National Food for Work Programme (NFFWP), whichever is in force in that area, shall be deemed to be the action plan for the Scheme for the purposes of the Act. These Guidelines have been formulated to facilitate the design and implementation of Rural Employment Guarantee Schemes. They should be interpreted as a broad operational framework, around which further provisions may be built, taking into account the State's economic, social and institutional context.

The Act is a Centrally Sponsored Scheme on a cost sharing basis between the Centre and the States. The Central Government will bear all costs, other than the following:

— 25 per cent of the cost of material and wages for semi-skilled/skilled workers;
— Unemployment allowance; and
— Administrative expenses of the State Employment Guarantee Council.

PLANNING

Planning is of critical importance for successful implementation of the REGS. The basic aim of the planning process is to ensure that the District is prepared well in advance to offer productive employment on demand. The need to get within a definite time period necessities advance planning. A key-indicator of success is the timely generation of employment within 15 days. Simultaneously, it is also necessary that design and selection of works are such that high quality assets are developed[10].

The Programme officer is responsible for matching the demand for work in the Block with the employment opportunities arising from the REGS projects. For this purposes, he is to prepare a plan for the Block by consolidating the proposals of the Gram Panchayats and Intermediate Panchayats according to Section 15 (3) of NREGA.

The District Programme Co-ordinator is also required to prepare a 'Labour Budget' by the end of December for the next financial year. The Labour budget should have the details of anticipated demand for unskilled manual work in the District, and the Plan for engaging of labourers in REGS works. It is to be submitted to the District Panchayat[11].

Annual Plan should be seen as a part of a long-term strategy for sustainable employment generation in the District. The need to integrate work priorities with a longer-term development strategy demands 'creation of durable assets and strengthening of the livelihood resource base of the rural poor. It is suggested, therefore, that Districts develop perspective plans to enable them to assess the causal factors of poverty and possible intervention. The state council is expected to prepare a list of preferred work for different areas based on their ability to create durable assets.

DISTRICT PERSPECTIVE PLAN

District Perspective plan (DPP) is to facilitate advance planning. It provides a development perspective for the District. It is expected that it will identify the types of REGS works that should be encouraged in the districts and the possible linkages between these works and long-term employment generation for sustainable development[12].

A DPP of five years will have the advantages of facilitating annual working plans on the basis of which annual budgets can be estimated and drawn up, and also give a continuum to plan works beyond the restriction of a financial year. The DPP is to serve as a framework of long-term planning. But is will be flexible enough to respond to the new emerging needs of the area, experience of execution and the new works approved by Central Government[13].

The DPP generally, has the following important features[14]:

— Village based: with the village as the unit for planning
— Holistic: Cover socio-economic aspects of development
— Diagnostic: include a causal analysis of poverty. This will identify gaps and needs and indicate the nature of inputs required.
— Delineates baselines
— Indicate outcome based strategies
— Indicate methods for measurement of customers; and
— Map resources

DPP will also facilitate an inter-sectoral approach, so that Districts can address certain fundamental causes of poverty in the area. If the DPP has been made under NFFWP, it should be revised in order to serve the purpose of NREGA. The draft plan should be discussed and approved by the Gram Sabha, Gram Panchayat, Intermediate Panchayat and District Panchayat. Efforts should be made to ensure the participation of those who are likely to seek work under the Act in the village. Their demand for work as well as their preference for the nature and time of work should be learnt, so that the Plan may be able to provide them employment according to their need. Every village should develop its Perspective Plan so that it can add value to the works associated with the NREGS.

THE ANNUAL PLAN

The annual plan is basically the working plan which identifies the activities to be taken up on priority in a year. The Perspective plan, however, is required to provide the framework for facilitating this identification. In case of the activities to be taken up, their justification should be indicated in terms of needs and outcomes.

The Gram Panchayat is required to convene meeting of the Gram Sabha to estimate the demand for labour every year, and to propose the number and priority of works to be undertaken in the next financial year. The timing of the meeting should take into consideration the work season and the migration time. Participation of likely beneficiaries should be ensured in the Gram Sabha so that their priorities and needs shape the Annual Plan. The time and date of the Gram Sabha meeting should be decided well in advance and be widely published so that people can participate in maximum numbers[15].

The recommendations noted in the Gram Sabha should be forwarded to the Gram Panchayat. It will prepare an Annual Plan on the basis of such recommendation and forward it to the Programme Officer. The annual plan should show clearly, the existing demand for work, the demand in the previous year, the works taken up in the previous year, ongoing works and works proposed for the next year, likely costs and the proposed Implementing Agencies. Of course, the Gram Panchayat should also identify the 50 per cent of the works in its area that it may like to take up.

The Programme Officer is responsible for scrutinising the Annual Plan for making it technically feasible. He should satisfy himself that it meets the likely demand for the employment based on registrations and previous experience. Further, he is required to ascertain that the employment opportunities arising from the projects in the area under his jurisdiction match the demand for employment. If the Programme Officer feels that the list is not sufficient enough to meet the likely demand, he can ask for a supplementary list[16].

The Programme Officer should not reject a proposal received from the Gram Panchayat. If the proposal is not within the provisions of the Act, or does not appear technically feasible, he is required to record his observations on the proposal and then submit a consolidated statement of proposals to the Intermediate Panchayat. Also, the Intermediate Panchayat will not reject a work proposed by the Gram Panchayat, if it is within the parameters of the Act. In case, it is outside the parameters of the Act, then it will be returned to the Gram Panchyat for this body to replace it with valid proposal[17].

The Intermediate Panchyat is needed to maintain the priority indicated by the Gram Panchyat. It is also possible that there may be a need for works that involve more than one Gram Panchayat. Such type of works may be included by the Intermediate Panchayat. The priority of works in a Gram Panchayat will be decided by the Gram Panchayat. Further, based on these recommendations, the Plan for area of the Intermediate Panchayat should be approved by the Intermediate Panchayat and forwarded to the District Program Coordinator[18].

The District Programme Coordinator is required to scrutinize the plan proposals of all the Intermediate Panchyats examining the appropriateness and adequacy of works in terms of likely demand as well as their technical and financial feasibility. He should also invite and review work proposals from other implementing agencies but in doing so the priorities of Gram Panchayat and the priorities of inter Gram Panchayat need to be condered as these are. Moreover, he should also consolidate all these proposals into District Plan proposal to be discussed and approved by the District Panchayat. The time frame for each Project must be clearly specified in the annual plan. The District Plan should comprise a block wise shelf of projects, arranged Gram Panchayat-wise. The Implementing Agency for each work has to be identified keeping in view the minimum of 50 per cent of works to be executed by Gram Panchayat as required by the Act. Lastly, it may be mentioned that the District Panchayat is required to review and approve the District Plan[19].

The District Programme Coordinator is required to coordinator the preparation of detailed technical estimates as well as sanctions. The Project report of every approved work should contain complete details as may be stated in the technical/work manual of the State Governments. It should also clarify the expected outcomes like person days of employment, specifications of the physical assets (e.g. length of road, size of tank) and long-lasting outcomes (e.g. area irrigated, villages connected).

The District Programme Coordinator is required to communicate the sanctioned Plan to the Programme Officer. The Programme Officer should forward a copy of the Block Plan, with the shelf of projects to be executed in each Gram Panchayat as well as projects that may be inter Gram Panchayat. These plans should contain project cost, time frame, person-days to be generated and the name of Implementing Agency. Planning for projects must give priority to low-wage areas, where the demand for work at minimum wages is likely to be high. This entire process should be completed by the December of the preceding year. Lastly, the State Government should fix the time-frame for each level to propose, examine and the approve works should be widely publicized subsequently[20].

REGISTRATION AND EMPLOYMENT (ELIGIBILITY)

The Rural Employment Guarantee Scheme (NREGS) has to be open to all rural households in the areas notified by the Central Government. The entitlement of 100 days of guaranteed employment in a financial year is in terms of a household. This entitlement of 100 days per year can be shared within the household; more than one person in a household can be employed simultaneously or at different times. Adult members of the household who register may apply for work. In order to register they have to[21]:

— be local residents, local means within Gram Panchayat. This includes migrant families of that area, including those that may have migrated sometime ago but may return.

— be wiling to do unskilled manual work

— apply as a household at the local Gram Panchayat.

APPLICATION FOR REGISTRATION

Application for registration may be given on plain paper to the local Gram Panchayat. However, it should contain the names of those adult members of the household who are willing to do unskilled manual work, and particulars such as age, sex and SC/ST states. The state Government may make a printed form available to the applicant, but an application on a printed form is not necessary[22].

— An individual may appear personally and make an oral request for registration.

— Verification of applications will be regarding local residence in the Gram Panchyat concerned and that applicants are adult members of the household.

— A Gram Sabha shall be convened when the Act commences the purpose of the Gram Sabha will be to explain the provisions of the Act, mobilize applications for registrations and conduct verifications.

— A door to door survey may be undertaken to identify person willing to register under the Act. The Survey may be conducted by a team headed by the President of Gram Panchayat and involving ward members, SC/ST women residents, a village level government functionary and the Gram Panchayat secretary, the team members may be given orientation at the Block/District level.

- To allow maximum opportunities to familes that may migrate, registration will be open throughout the year at the Gram Panchayat office during working hours.
- The process of verification shall be completed as early as possible, and in any case, not later than a fortnight after the receipt of the application in the Gram Panchayat.
- After verification, the Gram Panchayat will enter all details in the Registration in the Gram Panchayat.
- Every registered household will be assigned a unique registration number.
- Copies of the registration are to be sent to the Programme Officer for the purpose of reporting to the Intermediate Panchayat and District Panchayat for further planning, tracking and recording.
- A Gram Sabha of registered workers must be convened.
- If a person who applies for registration and provides incorrect information regarding his/her name, residence or adult status, he/she will become ineligible. In such cases, the Gram Panchyat will refer the matter to the Programme Officer. The Programme Officer, after independent verification of facts may give the concerned person an opportunity to be heard. He may also direct the Gram Panchayat to cancel his registration and job card.
- Such cancellation lists should be made public and should be presented to the Gram Sabha.

JOB CARDS

The Gram Panchayat is required to issue the jobcards to every registered household. This is an important legal document and helps in ensuring transparency besides protecting labourers against fraud. The job cards should be issued immediately after verifications, i.e. within a fortnight of the application for registration. These should be issued in the presence of the local community.

Photographs of adult members who are applicants have to be attached to the job cards. The cost of the job cards, including that of photographer, is the part of the programme cost. The State Government in a particular area may order the photograph to be affixed later (within three months) if the arrangement of the photograph is not possible immediately. A copy of the job card has to be maintained at the Gram Panchayat also.

The job card is valid for a period of five years. It will have provision for addition/deletion of members eligible for work. Deletions in any household on account of demise, or permanent change of residence of a member, are to be reported immediately by the household concerned. Request for additions desired may be made for by the household. The Gram Panchayat should also undertake an annual updating exercise in the same manner as registration, the time for which should be fixed keeping in mind the work and seasonal migration of the local workforce[23].

All additions and deletions made in the Registration Register should be read out in the Gram Sabha and than the Gram Panchayat should send a list of additions/deletions to the Programme Officer. Job card should contain permanent information regarding the household as well as the employment details for five years. Permanent information will include the household registration number and particulars (age and sex) of all adult members of the family who show willingness to work.

The basic features of NREGA may be printed on its other side of the job cards to create wider awareness of the Act. A cardholder may apply for a duplicate job card to the Gram Panchayat if the original card is lost or damaged. In case, a person has any grievance against the non-issuance of a job card, he or she may bring the matter to the notice of the concerned Programme Officer. If the grievance is against the Programme Officer, he/she may bring it to the notice of the District Programmes Coordinator or the designated grievance – redressal authority at the Block or District level. However, all such complaints shall be disposed off within 15 days[24].

APPLICATION FOR WORK

The application for seeking work should be submitted to the Gram Panchayat. Workers should have the option of submitting an application directly to the Programme Officer, but this should be treated as 'fall back' option only. Application should be submitted in writing on plain paper, stating:

— The registration number of the job card
— The date from which employment is required and
— The number of days of employment required.

One application may be given for a number of days in different periods during the year for which employment is needed. Besides, 'Joint Applications' may also be submitted by several applicants. A dated receipt for the application for work must be issued to the applicant. Information on new applications for work should be communicated at least once a week by the Gram Panchayat to the Programme Officer. At the same time, the Gram Panchayat should also specify how many of the new applicants are being employed on "Panchayat works' (and for how long), and how many are to be provided employment on 'general works' by the Programme Officer[25].

ALLOCATION OF EMPLOYMENT OPPORTUNITIES

According to Schedule I, Section 10 of NREGA, the Programme Officer and Gram Panchayat are required to direct any person who has applied for employment to do work of any type permissible under the Act. The State Government needs to establish clear coordination mechanisms so that data on work requests allotted by the Porgramme Officer and Gram Panchayat are properly maintained. This information should be recorded on the job card and the employment register as well. Both the agencies should share information on employment allotted and works started.

If few applicants have to be given the work beyond 5 Kms of their residence, women (especially single women) and older persons should be given preference to work on the worksites nearer to their residence. The work entitlement of 100 days per household per year may be shared between different adult members of the same household. If several members of a household who share the same job card are employed at the same time under the scheme they should be allowed to work on the same worksite.

In case unusual circumstances appear and members have to be allocated work on different worksites, the Gram Panchayat should ensure that job cards are duly processed at both worksites. If the Gram Panchayat decides it cannot be given under its own shelf of works, and that employment needs to be given outside the Gram Panchayat it will communicate to the Programme Officer. When the Programme Officer receives this information from the Gram Panchayat, he will allot work. Such work will be selected from the shelf of projects that include inter-Gram Panchayat works. The Programme Officer will also inform the Gram Panchayat concerned about the employment allotted so that the employment data are consolidated in Employment Register at the Gram Panchayat.

If anybody requests for employment is made to the Programme Officer and he allots work, he must inform the Gram Panchayat so that the data on works and employment are coordinated at that level too. The Gram Panchayat will also inform the Programme Officer of the employment allotments made. Such information sharing exercise should be done on a prescribed porforma every week.

Applicants receiving work will be intimated by the Gram Panchayat/Programme Officer by means of a letter sent to them at the address provided in the job cards, and also by a public notice displayed at the offices of the Gram Panchayat and Programme Officer[26].

Scheduled II, Section 6 requires that priority will be given to women in such a way that at least one third of the beneficiaries shall be women who have registered and requested for work. In case a rural disabled person applied for work, work suitable to his/her ability and qualifications will have to be given. This may also be in the form of services that are relevant to the programme. Provisions of Person with Disabilities (Equal opportunities, Protection of Right and full participation) Act 1995 will be kept in view and implemented. Schedule II, Section 6 entrusts the Programme Officer with the responsibility of ensuring that every applicant is provided unskilled work. Thus, the overall responsibility of coordination and resource support to the Gram Panchayat and other implementing agencies will remain with the Programme Officer. So as to ensure that every applicant has work according to the legal entitlement; the Programme Officer shall have the power to supervise and direct the Gram Panchayats and other implementing agencies to discharge their responsibilities.

In case any implementing agency fails to do so, the Programme Officer will have to ensure that applicants for work are not aggrieved and make arrangements for their employment. He is required to report the matter to the District Programme Coordinator for necessary action.

TIME BOUND EMPLOYMENT

The Gram Panchayat/Programme officer will be responsible for providing wage employment to the applicant within 15 days of the date of receipt of the application. If applications are submitted in advance, employment will be provided from the date that the employment has been sought, or within 15 days of the date of applications, whichever is later. If any Gram Panchayat is not to provide employment within 15 days it will be the responsibility of the Programme Officer to do so. The employment allotted by the Programme Officer will be communicated to the Gram Panchayat and vice versa.

In case an implementing agency directed by the Programme Officer, does not start begin on time, or does not employ the persons directed to it for work by the Gram Panchayat, the Programme Officer will make alternative arrangements to ensure employment for such applicants[27].

According to Section 14 (d) of the Act, the District Programme Coordinator will coordinate with the Programme Officers and the implementing agencies to ensure that applicants are provided employment as per their entitlement. If a Programme Officer is unable to provide employments the District Programme Coordinator will intervene to make appropriate arrangements for employment.

RECORD OF EMPLOYMENT

Every agency paying wages must record on the job card the amount paid and the number of days for which payment has been made. A copy of the master roll of every work should be sent by the Programme Officer to those Gram Panchayats from where workers are employed and in whose jurisdiction the work is done. The Gram Panchayat will consolidate household-wise employment data in the employment register. The responsibility for coordination of employment data will be with the Gram Panchayat at Gram Panchayat level, and with the Programme Officer at the block level. Hence, a system for timely sharing of information between these two levels has to be ensured. The Programme Officer, however, will be responsible for ensuring that this coordination remains functional[28].

PERMISSIBLE WORKS

In accordance with Schedule I of the Act, the focus of the Rural Employment Guarantee Scheme shall be on the following works:

— Water conservation and water harvesting;

— Drought proofing, including afforestation and tree plantation;

— Irrigation canals, including micro and minor irrigation works;

— Provision of irrigation facility to land owned by households belonging to SC/ST, or to land of the beneficiaries of land reforms, or to land of the beneficiaries under Indira Awas Yojana;

— Renovation of traditional water bodies, including de-sitting of tanks;

— Land development;

— Flood-control and protection works, including drainage in waterlogged areas;

— Rural connectivity to provide all-weather access. The construction of roads may include culverts where necessary and within the village area may be taken up along with drains;

— Any other work that may be notified by the Central Government in consultation with the state government.

IMPLEMENTATION PRINCIPLES

The effective implementation of NREGA involves, first and foremost, ensuring that the demand for employment is met on time, that workers receive their due entitlements, and that there is proper planning and supervision of works. In order to achieve this objective, the National Rural Employment Guarantee

Act has *six basic implementation principles*[29]. These are:

1. Collaborative Partnerships and Public Accountability

The fundamental consideration of this Act is a collaborative partnership among Central Government, the State Governments, the Panchayat and the local community. In fact, the main implementation activities are at the village and block levels, while coordination activities are mainly at the Block and District Levels. However, planning, supervision and monitoring take place at all levels and at each level concerned people are accountable to the community.

2. Community Participation

The second principle of implementation of the Act is the statutorily mandated institutional mechanism at village level (Gram Sabha) for community participation. Besides this other methods — local vigilance, monitoring committees, workers' associations, local beneficiary committees, SHGs user groups and other gross-root structures could also be evolved. It is important the community participation for ensuring transparency and public accountability.

3. Role of Panchayats

The Panchyats at each level will be the Principal Authorities for planning and implementation of the schemes under the section 13(1) of the Act.

4. District Programme Coordinator and Programme Officer

These authorities share the overall responsibility for ensuring that the scheme is implemented according to the Act. District Programme Coordinator belongs to the District level while the Programme Officer functions at the Block level.

5. Coordination among the agencies

The Panchayats at different levels will need to coordinate with each other for the proper implementation of the Act. Likewise, the Panchyats and the District/Block Administration will have to work together.

6. Resource Support

The Central and the State Governments will facilitate the implementation of the Act through timely and adequate resource support.

CAPACITY BUILDING AND AWARENESS

All the major agencies of vital importance need to be trained in discharging their responsibilities under the Act. This will include Gram Panchayats, other PRIs, District and State level department personnel involved in implementing REGS, local committees formed for the purpose of vigilance, monitoring and social audit. The state government is supposed to arrange training on core issues relevant to the Act to its key functionaries, particularly the District Programme Co-ordinator, the Programme officer and PRIs. The priority will be given to impart training on the issues related to effective planning, work measurement, public disclosure, social audits and use of the Right to Information Act, 2005.

COMMUNICATION OF NREGA AND THE REGS

It is essential for the people to know their rights under the Act, because effective communication of information about the Act and the scheme is also important. The basic features of the Act and the

Scheme should be widely published in local languages. The marginalised communities and deprived areas should be given priority. Aspects of critical importance enshrined in the Act like, process of registration and application, the entitlements of REGS workers, social audits, grievance redressal procedures and the different agencies must be communicated in simple language clearly. Local cultural forms and intensive interpersonal communication such as discussions and meetings should be organized to generate awareness on regular basis.

The effectiveness of this communication process will certainly make impact on the people who need work under this Act, register and apply for work. Further, active involvement of local communities at every stage, prompt grievance redressal, vigilant social audits by the Gram Sabhas, and use of right to information are some of other indicators of successful communication. Having all said and done, the communication process is required to be designed to help people in making their demands and claim their legal entitlements[30].

We have described the basic objective and major features of the National Rural Employment Guarantee Act, 2005 (NREGA) and its implementation mechanism in accordance with the Act. As stated earlier, we have heavily drawn on NREGA (2005) and Operational Guidelines prepared by the Ministry of Rural Development, Government of India in this Chapter. The Act is now applicable to all the districts of the country. However, for our research study, we have confined only to four selected districts out of twenty two identified backward districts of UP in the first phase of NRGEA implementation. In the next Chapter, we have briefly presented the social, economic and administrative contours of the study area i.e. Uttar Pradesh.

REFERENCES

1 The Gazette of India, Extraordinary (Part II), Section 1, Ministry of Law and Justice, Legislative Department, September 7, 2005.

2 NREGA Section 2

3 NREGA Operational Guidelines, 2006, Ministry of Rural Development, Department of Rural Development, Government of India, p.7.

4 Ibid, p.6

5 NREGA Section 12

6 op.cit., p.5

7 Ibid.

8 Ibid., p.4

9 NREGA, Section 20; op.cit. pp.30-31

10 Op.cit.p. 9

11 Ibid.

12 Ibid., p. 10

13 Ibid

14 Ibid.

15 Ibid. p. 11

16 Ibid. p. 12

17 Ibid.

18 Ibid.

19 Ibid.

20 Ibid., pp. 12-13

21 Ibid., p.14; NREGA Schedule II

22 Ibid., p. 15

23 op.cit., p. 16

24 Ibid., pp.16-17

25 Ibid., p. 17

3
Profile of Study Area : Uttar Pradesh

This chapter presents the demographic, social and economic and administrative contours of the study area. The profile includes socio-economic and demographic characteristics of state, districts, villages and households.

I. STUDY AREA: UTTAR PRADESH

Uttar Pradesh, also known as the "Hindi speaking heartland" of India, is the fifth largest state. The State covers 240928 sq.kms and accounts for 7.3 percent of total area of the country, while its share in country's population is 16.2 percent. U.P. is organized into 70 districts, 300 *tehsils* and 813 development blocks. There are 52028 village *panchayats* in the State covering 97134 inhabited villages. The majority of U.P.'s villages are small, with an average population of around 3194 per *panchayat.* As in other parts of India, land is the single most important resource of livelihood. The per capita availability of land has been low and it stood at a meagre 0.10 hectare in 2001-02. The State is rich in surface and ground water resources. Over three-fourth of the sown area is irrigated mostly through tubewells. U.P. also has a fairly large canal network. The profile includes demographic, social and economic characteristics of State (Box 3.1.) and

Box 3.1: Profile of Study Area: Uttar Pradesh

Population	(2001)	16.62 crore
Geographical area	(2001)	2.41 lakh sq. km.
Population density	(2001)	689 per sq.km.
Sex Ratio	(2001)	898
Share of SC/ST Population		23.77%
OBC Population		34.53%
Upper Caste (Hindu)Population		24.53%
Muslim Population		16.7%
Literacy Rate	(2001)	Male: 57.36% Female: 42.98
Net State Domestic Product	(2001-02)	9753

Percentage share in total workers (2001)		Percentage share in State Income(2002-03)	
1. Agriculture	66.0	1. Agriculture	31.8
2. House hold Indu.	6.0	2. Manufacturing	10.9
3. Other services	28.0		

Poverty Rate (1999-2000)	31%
Unemployment Rate (1999-2000)	4.48%

Source : Compiled from Human Development Report 2003: Uttar Pradesh

for districts and sample villages see Annexures.

Demographic Profile

The State's demography is marked by persistent increase in population which has more than doubled since 1951. The total fertility rate in U.P. was as high as 6.9 in 1972. It declined to 6.0 in 1982 and further to 5.6 in 1992. Thus, the total decline during this 20-year period was only 19 per cent, while the decrease in population at All India Level was 28 per cent. The fertility rate in U.P. is highest among all States and double of fertility rate in Kerala. The sex ratio stood at 898 in 2001 and children below 7 years constituted

19.03 percent of total population. The birth rate in U.P. was as high as 54.6 in 1971. It decreased to 39.6 in 1981 and further to 35.7 in 1991. It presently stands at the high level of 31.6. The adverse sex ratio, high fertility and mortality rates, a high proportion of children and a slow process of demographic change lead slow social development in the State.

Social Profile

In Uttar Pradesh as compared to other parts of India, there are diverse religious and social groups. According to 2001 Census, the Scheduled Castes and Tribes constituted about 21.1 percent and 0.1 percent of the total population respectively. The religious minorities were 18.5 percent and the Muslims alone accounted for 17.7 percent of the population. Estimates of population based on the National Sample Survey of 1999-00 (55th Round) showed that Hindus belonging to upper and intermediate castes were 22.73 percent of the State's population, while Other Backward Classes and Schedule Caste/Tribes constituted 35.52 percent and respectively.

Economic Profile

The State's per capita income has been close to the national average during early period of Independence during 1950-51. However, over the entire period of the Five Year Plans the gap between U.P.'s per capita income and the national per capita income has steadily increased. In 2001-02 the per capita income in U.P. was Rs. Rs. 9753, which is 45.7 percent lower than the national average of Rs. 17947. While U.P.'s rate of growth quickened in the 1980s, it declined significantly during the 1990s. U.P.'s rate of growth at 4.2 percent per annum during the period 1991-2001 was significantly lower than the national average, ranking tenth among the 15 major states. There are significant regional variations also. For instance, some of the districts in western U.P. enjoy higher levels of income than those in other regions (Government of Utter Pradesh 2007[1]).

Another striking feature of the State would be the category of high incident poverty States. In 1993-94 the State ranked 11th out of the 14 major States of India in poverty levels with 36 per cent of persons below the poverty line. Both rural and urban poverty declined in U.P. over the years though, year-to-year fluctuations and continue to greater concentration of the country's poor in Uttar Pradesh. A staggering 6050 lakh persons in U.P. were living in poverty in 1993-94 constituting the largest concentration of the poor anywhere in the world.

State-wide trends in poverty reveal that there is a wide variation in the level of poverty across U.P.'s regions and social groups. In 1993-94, the Southern region (Bundelkhand) had the highest level of poverty – more than two-and-a-half time the level in the Himalayan region (now Uttaranchal) and more than that in the Eastern region, traditionally considered to have high levels of poverty. Similarly, among caste groups, the Scheduled Castes, Tribes and Other Backward class population living in poverty higher than that of other castes population. The incidence of poverty appears comparatively higher among the SC/ST households than non-SC/ST households. According to the World Bank report, the probability of a Scheduled Caste/Tribe household being poor in the state was 1.5 times than the non-SC/ ST households in 1987-88. In 1993-94 and 1999-00, this probability had increased to 1.6 times. In the urban areas, a SC/ ST household was 1.8 times likelier to be poor compared to other households in 1993-94 (World Bank, 2002[2]).

II. PROFILES OF SELECTED DISTRICTS

The present study has been carried out in the four districts, namely, Barabanki, Raebareli, Sitapur and Unnao from among 22 districts of U. P. identified during the first phase of selection of the most backward districts in the country for implementation of National Rural Employment Guarantee Act, 2005. We, therefore, present a brief profile of each selected district.

1. District Barabanki

The district Barabanki spread over the area of 4558 sq km is about 29 kms afar from Lucknow, the capital of U. P. in the east. Barabanki, being one of the four district of Faizabad division is located between 2630' North and 2719' North and longitudes 8058' East and 8155' East. The district is surrounded by the district Faizabad in the East, district Gonda and Bahraich in the North East, district Sitapur in the North West, district Lucknow in the West, district Raebareli in the South and district Sultanpur in the South East. The district comprises of six administrative sub divisions and seventeen development blocks. There are 1821 villages and 1139 gram panchayats in the district.

It may also mention that the Scheduled Castes population formed 27 percent of the total population in the district. There are 6.65 lakh rural households which cover 31.31 lakh population in Barabanki district. Out of the total households, 47.21% households having 3.14 lakh population constitute below poverty line families. The important facts about the district Barabanki are mentioned in the Box No. 3.2

Box 3.2 : District of Barabanki – Important Facts

1. Geographical Area – 4558 sq.km.
2. Population (2001): -

Persons	–	2673581
Male	–	1416921
Female	–	1256660
Urban	–	248745
Rural	–	2424836

1. Decennial Growth Rate (1991 – 2001) – 26.4
2. Density – 699 Persons /sq. km.
3. Sex Ratio – 887 Females per 1000 males.
4. S. C. Population – 718897

Male	–	380469
Female	–	338428

5. S. T. Population – 456

Male	–	235
Female	–	221

6. Literacy Rate (religion wise): -

Hindu	–	48.98%
Muslims	–	41.38%
Christians	–	51.53%
Sikhs	–	59.83%
Buddhists	–	42.98%
Jains	–	94.49%

Source: Uttranchal and Uttar Pradesh at a glance – 2005, District - wise Statistical Overview, Jagran Research Centre, Kanpur

2. District Raebareli

Raebareli is one of the six districts of the Lucknow division. It is situated between atitude 2536' North and Longitude 10041' East and 8134' East. It is bounded by Tehsil Mohanlalganj of district Lucknow and Haidergarh of district Barabanki on the North, on the East by Tehsil Mussafirkhana of district Sultanpur and on the South West by Pratapgarh. The Suothern boundary is formed by the

Box 3.3 : District Raebareli Important Facts

Arca – 4586 sq.km.		
1. Administrative Units: -		
Statutory Towns	–	9
Tehsils	–	7
Villages	–	1733
Block	–	21
Gram Panchayat	–	965
2. Population : -		
Total	–	2872335
Male	–	1472230
Female	–	1400105
Urban	–	273998
Rural	–	2598337
3. Decennial Growth Rate – 23.66%		
4. Density – 626 Persons /sq. km.		
5. Sex Ratio – 961 Females per 1000 males.		
6. S. C. Population – 856749		
Male	–	436161
Female	–	421588
7. S. T. Population – 1802		
Male	–	937
Female	–	875
8. Literacy Rate (religion wise): -		
Hindu	–	54.24%
Muslims	–	49.98%
Christians	–	67.24%
Sikhs	–	82.29%
Buddhists	–	81.55%
Jains	–	92.59%

Source : Uttranchal and Uttar Pradesh at a glance – 2005, District - wise Statistical Overview, Jagran Research Centre, Kanpur river Ganga which separates it from the district Fatehpur. On the West side lies the Purawa Tehsil of district Unnao.

District Raebareli has seven sub-divisions namely, Raebareli, Dalmau, Mahrajganj, Salon, Lalganj, Tiloi and Unchahar. A Chief Development Officer looks after all the development work to be executed in the district. While there is a District Development Officer at the District headquarters, each development block is headed by a Block Development officer like in any other district of the state. There are twenty one Development Blocks in Raebareli district.

The climate of Raebareli district is almost dry. Annual rainfall is about 900 – 1000 m.m. which is mainly during the period of July to September. Paddy is the main Kharif crop and wheat is the main Rabi crop in the district. It may also be mentioned that sugarcane and potato are the main cash crops of the district.

3. District Sitapur

Situated on the bank of river 'Sarayan' along Lucknow – Delhi National Highway only 89 km. from the State's capital, Lucknow. Sitapur has six administrative divisions namely, Sitapur, Biswan, Mishrikh, Laharpur, Mahmoodabad and Sidhauli. It has 19 blocks, 2 parliamentary constituencies viz. Sitapur and Mishrikh (Scheduled Castes) and 9 assembly constituencies namely, Behta, Biswan, Mahmoodabad, Sidhauli (S. C.), Laharpur, Sitapur, Hargaon (S. C.), Mishrikh and Machhrehta (S. C.). The meter gauge Railway line from Lucknow to Bareilly via Lakhimpur – Kheri and Pilibhit districts is connected to this city. Besides this, Sitapur is also connected on broad gauge train network to Gorakhpur district and

Box 3.4 : District Sitapur Important Facts

	Sitapur		
1.	Area	–	5743 sq.km.
2.	Administrative Units: -		
	Statutory Towns	–	11
	Tehsils	–	6
	Villages	–	2321
	Block	–	19
	Gram Panchayat	–	1326
3.	Population : -		
	Total	–	3619661
	Male	–	1941374
	Female	–	1678287
	Urban	–	432688
	Rural	–	3186973
4.	Decennial Growth Rate	–	26.58%
5.	Density	–	630 Persons /sq. km.
6.	Sex Ratio	–	864 Females per 1000 males.
7.	S. C. Population	–	1153626
	Male	–	619501
	Female	–	534125
8.	S. T. Population	–	367
	Male	–	191
	Female	–	176
9.	Literacy Rate (religion wise): -		
	Hindu	–	54.24%
	Muslims	–	49.98%
	Christians	–	67.24%
	Sikhs	–	82.29%
	Buddhists	–	81.65%
	Jains	–	92.59%

Source: Uttranchal and Uttar Pradesh at a glance – 2005, District - wise Statistical Overview, Jagran Research Centre, Kanpur

Delhi via Gonda, Burhwal bypassing Lucknow and Hardoi. The district is spread over the area of 5743 sq. kms., and populated by 36.19 lakh persons.

4. District Unnao

District Unnao, a part of Lucknow division, is situated between the cities of Lucknow and Kanpur. It is bounded on the North by district Hardoi, on the East by district Lucknow, on the South by district Raebareli and on the West by the river Ganga, it has produced many renowned freedom fighters, poets and political leaders. It assumed its present size in 1869.

Unnao district comprises of five Tehsils namely, Hasanganj, Safipur, Purawa and Bighapur. It has sixteen development blocks viz. Ganj Moradabad, Bangarman, Fatehpur Chaurasi, Safipur, Miyanganj, Auras, Hasanganj, Nawabganj, Purva, Asoha, Hilauli, Bighapur, Sumerpur, Bichhia, Sikandarpur Sirausi and Sikanderpur Karan.

Topographically the Unnao Industrial Area is conducive for industrial enterprises. It is almost free from residential habitation and linked with roadways, railways as well as airport. The nationalized commercial banks, and financial institutions like Industrial Development Bank of India, U. P. State Finance Corporation are located within the radius of 40 to 60 kms. (at Kanpur and Lucknow). The Reserve Bank of India is also situated at the nearby city of Kanpur. Tanneries are the major industry in Unnao. This district is also famous for its leather goods. Most of the enterprises mainly in leather segment are export oriented units.

III. DEMOGRAPHIC PROFILE OF SELECTED VILLAGES

Box 3.5 : District Unnao: Important Facts

Unnao			
1.	Area	–	4558 sq.km.
2.	Administrative Units: -		
	Tehsils	–	5
	Villages	–	1689
	Block	–	16
	Gram Panchayat	–	983
3.	Population : -		
	Total	–	2700324
	Male	–	1422509
	Female	–	1277815
	Urban	–	411543
	Male	–	216857
	Female	–	194666
	Rural	–	2288781
	Male	–	1205652
	Female	–	1083129
4.	Decennial Growth Rate	–	22.72%
5.	Density	–	592 Persons /sq. km.
6.	Sex Ratio	–	898 Females per 1000 males.
7.	S. C. Population	–	827256
	Male	–	432367
	Female	–	394888
8.	Literacy Rate (religion wise): -		
	Male	–	51.6%
	Female	–	23.6%
	Hindu	–	55.25%
	Muslims	–	49.50%
	Christians	–	57.17%
	Sikhs	–	67.12%
	Buddhists	–	45.48%
	Jains	–	74.39%

Source: Uttranchal and Uttar Pradesh at a glance – 2005, District - wise Statistical Overview, Jagran Research Centre, Kanpur

After having described the brief profiles of the four selected districts in Uttar Pradesh, we present here the available data related to the demographic profiles of selected sixteen villages where the workers at various sites were interviewed.

1. Village: Alapur; Block: Banki; District: Barabanki.

There are 229 households in the village. Out of these 97 households, (i.e. 42%) are below the poverty line. According to the information provided by the village development officer, the number of households belonging to the other backward castes is highest, (i.e. 98%). While the households belonging to scheduled castes and the general category people are 76 and 45 respectively, the Muslim population lives in only 10 households. Alapur village has total population of 1206 persons. It may be mentioned that the percentage share of scheduled castes is the highest (46%) among all the castes. However, the OBCs and general category persons constitute 25% and 29% of the total population respectively.

2. Village: Piprauli; Block: Banki; District: Barabanki.

Spread over the area of 274.90 hectare, the village has 190.10 ha as total cultivable area. There are 321 households in Piprauli, of which 127 households, i.e. 40% are below poverty line. In the total population of 1578 persons, 462 people (29%) belong to scheduled castes. About 47% people are literate in this village. However, the literacy rate among women is around 31% and 69% among the men.

3. Village: Kasimganj; Block: Dewa; District:

Barabanki.

Kasimganj has 238 households of which 104 households (44%) are living below poverty line. The total population of 1419 is shared by 27% scheduled castes, 68% other backward castes and 5% people in General category.

4. Village: Khajurgaon; Block: Dewa; District: Barabanki.

Village Khajurgaon is inhabited by 284 households. The number of households living below poverty line is 140, (i.e. 49%). Its total population is 1632 persons which comprises of 21% scheduled castes, 49% other backward castes and 30% people in General category.

The integrated aforementioned data relating to these villages in district Barabanki may be presented as follows: -

Table 3.1. Demographic Profiles of Selected Villages in District Barabanki

Villages → *Particulars ↓*	*Vill.: Alapur Block: Banki*	*Vill.: Piprauli Block: Banki*	*Vill.: Kasimganj Block: Dewa*	*Vill.: Khajurgaon Block: Dewa*
Total Households	229	321	238	284
S.C. Households	76 (33%)	NA	NA	100 (35%)
O.B.C. Households	98 (43%)	NA	NA	49 (17%)
General Households	45 (20%)	NA	NA	135 (48%)
Muslim Households	10 (4%)	—	—	—
No. of BPL Households	**97 (42%)**	**127 (40%)**	**104 (44%)**	**140 (49%)**
Total Population	1206	1578	1419	1632
Female	593	759	666	755
Male	613	819	753	877
S. C.	561 (46%)	462 (29%)	373 (27%)	351 (21%)
O. B. C.	300 (25%)	NA	972 (68%)	796 (49%)

General	345 (29%)	NA	74 (5%)	485 (30%)
Muslim	——	——	——	——

Source: Village Development Officers of respective villages.

Note: SC means Scheduled Caste, OBC is Other Backward Caste and BPL is Below Poverty Line. Figures in brackets denote the percentage. NA denotes Data Not Available.

5. Village: Thulendi; Block: Bachharawan; District: Raebareli

Thulendi has 963 households of which 423 households, i.e. 44% belong to poverty line category. The number of scheduled castes households being 165 is lesser than that of other backward castes and General category households, which stand equal to each other, i.e. 356. The Muslims reside only in 86 households. As far as total population of the village is considered, a total of 5629 persons inhabit in these households. The scheduled castes people constitute 27%, other backward class persons 20% and General category people 53% of the total population.

6. Village: Rasulpur; Block: Bachharawan; District: Raebareli

There are 307 total households in this village. Rasulpur has a population of 1679 persons; of which 48% are scheduled castes, 14% other backward castes and 38% people belong to the General Category. There are 34% households living below poverty line.

7. Village: Kumharawan; Block: Shivagarh; District: Raebareli

The village Kumharawan having 327 households, is inhabited by 2098 persons. Its 44%, i.e. 143 households are below poverty line. Of its total population, 16% belong to the scheduled castes, 45% to other backward castes and 39% to General category people.

8. Village: Pipari; Block: Shivagarh; District: Raebareli

There are a total of 174 households in Pipari. It has 47% households which live below poverty line. Having population of 1093 persons only, it has 50% population of scheduled castes, 22% persons of other backward castes and 28% people in General category. The comprehensive presentation of data related to demographics in these villages of Raebareli is as follows:

Table 3.2. Demographic Profiles of Selected Villages in District Raebareli.

Villages → *Particulars ↓*	*Vill.: Thulendi Block: Bachha-rawan*	*Vill.: Rasulpur Block: Bachh-rawan*	*Vill.: Kumh-arawan Block: Shivagarh*	*Vill.: Pipari Block: Shivagarh*
Total Households	963	307	327	174
S.C. Household's	165 (17%)	NA	72 (22%)	87 (50%)
O. B. C. Households	356 (37%)	NA	100 (31%)	25 (14%)
General Households	356 (37%)	NA	136 (41%)	62 (36%)
Muslim Households	86 (9%)	NA	19 (6%)	——
No. of BPL Households	**423 (44%)**	**103 (34%)**	**143 (44%)**	**82 (47%)**
Total Population	5629	1679	2098	1093
Female	2687	797	1025	509
Male	2942	882	1073	584
S. C.	1525 (27%)	807 (48%)	336 (10%)	545 (50%)
O. B. C.	1140 (20%)	234 (14%)	945 (45%)	239 (22%)
General	2964 (53%)	638 (38%)	817 (39%)	309 (28%)
Muslim	——	——	——	——

Source: Village Development Officers of respective villages.

Note: SC means Scheduled Caste, OBC is Other Backward Caste and BPL is Below Poverty Line. Figures in brackets denote the percentage. NA denotes Data Not Available.

9. Village: Bari; Block: Sidhauli; District: Sitapur

In the village Bari, there are 1025 total households. The number of households which live below poverty line is 345, i.e. 34%. The caste-wise composition of the total households is as follows: -

(i) Scheduled Castes households - 29%.

(ii) Other Backward Castes households - 15%.

(iii) General Category households - 33%.

The Muslims live in 23% households in Bari. Inhabiting a population of 6893 persons, the village has following caste-wise distribution of its population.

(i) Scheduled Castes - 20%.

(ii) Other Backward Class - 38%.

(iii) General Category - 42%.

10. Village: Aladadpur; Block: Sidhauli; District: Sitapur

Aladadpur is inhabited by 117 households, out of these 45 households, i.e. 38% are living below poverty line. The share of scheduled castes households is 32% while the other backward castes live in 44% of the total households. There are only 21% households belonging to the General category people. There are only 3 households of Muslims. Its total population of 694 is shared by 20% of scheduled castes, 60% of other backward castes and 20% of the General category persons.

11. Village: Shamsapur; Block: Gondalaman; District: Sitapur

There are 422 households in Shamsapur. Out of

these, 203 households, i.e. 52% reel under the poverty line norm. The village has 50% households which belong to scheduled castes, 30% households to other backward castes and 20% to the General Category households. Its total population is 2162. The caste-wise authentic distribution of the population could not be available during the field survey.

12. Village: Khewuta; Block: Gondalaman; District: Sitapur

Khewuta having a total of 242 households, is populated by 1619 persons. The share of scheduled castes households in this village is 23%, while the other backward castes live in 35% households. The households of General category people are 42%. In other words, the village population comprises of 12% scheduled castes, 45% of other backward castes and 43% of General category people. Only 15% households are below poverty line in this village.

The integrated depiction of village level demographic information of the four villages selected for survey in district Sitapur may be as follows: -

Table 3.3. Demographic Profiles of Selected Villages in District Sitapur

Villages → *Particulars ↓*	*Vill.:* *Bari* *Block:* *Sidhauli*	*Vill.:* *Aladadpur* *Block:* *Sidhauli*	*Vill.:* *Shamsapur* *Block:* *Gondalaman*	*Vill.:* *Khewuta* *Block:* *Gondalaman*
	1025	117	422	242
S.C. Households	300 (29%)	38 (32%)	211 (50%)	56 (23%)
O.B.C. Households	158 (15%)	51 (43%)	125 (30%)	86 (36%)
General Households	335 (33%)	25 (22%)	86 (20%)	100 (41%)
Muslim Households	232 (23%)	3 (3%)	——	——
No. of BPL Households	**345 (34%)**	**45 (38%)**	**203 (52%)**	**37 (15%)**
Total Population	6893	69	2162	1619

Female	3253	305	956	751
Male	3640	389	1206	868
S. C.	1352 (20%)	134 (20%)	NA	201 (12%)
O. B. C.	2654 (38%)	423 (60%)	NA	725 (45%)
General	2887 (42%)	137 (20%)	NA	693 (43%)
Muslim	—	—	—	—

Source: Village Development Officers of respective villages.

Note: SC means Scheduled Caste, OBC is Other Backward Caste and BPL is Below Poverty Line. Figures in brackets denote the percentage. NA denotes Data Not Available.

13. Village: Mehndikhera; Block: Hasanganj; District: Unnao

Village Mehndikhera is a constituent of Alampur alias Latifpur alias Munnikhera Gram Panchayat in Hasanganj block of District Unnao. It has 387 households populating 1956 persons. Its 46% households are in below poverty line category. The caste-wise distribution of all the households in this village is as follows: -

(i) Scheduled Castes households - 37%.

(ii) Other Backward Class households - 35%.

(iii) General Category households - 25%.

(iv) Muslim Households - 3%.

As far as caste-wise population of Mehndikhera is concerned, it may be stated as hereunder: -

(i) Scheduled Castes persons - 55%.

(ii) Other Backward Class persons - 29%.

(iii) General Category persons - 16%.

14. Village: Hasanganj; Block: Hasanganj; District: Unnao

There are a total of 660 households of which 225 households, i.e. 34% live below poverty line. The caste-wise composition of total households in this village may be mentioned as follows: -

(i) Scheduled Castes households - 17%.

(ii) Other Backward Class households - 32%.

(iii) General Category households - 47%.

(iv) Muslim Households - 4%.

Hasanganj village has a population of 4200 persons and its caste-wise distribution shows that there are 24% Scheduled Castes, 36% Other Backward Castes and 40% General Category people.

15. Village: Khajuri; Block: Nawabganj; District: Unnao

Khajuri is a village among all the villages where we have visited to interview workers, which has the least number of households. There are only 37 households. This village falls under Bhiterepar Gram Panchayat of Nawabganj block. Out of 37 households, 12, i.e. 32% households are below poverty line, 57% households belong to scheduled castes and 43% to the General category households. There are none of the households belonging to either to Other Backward Castes or Muslims. The village has a population of 184 persons of which 70% are scheduled castes and 30% are General Category people.

16. Village: Tendua Hiran Kuddi; Block: Nawabganj; District: Unnao

Having a population of 1782 persons in 322 households the village has 48% households below poverty line. The caste-wise break-up of the total households is as follows: -

(i) Scheduled Castes - 18%.

(ii) Other Backward Class - 30%.

(iii) General Category - 49%.

(iv) Muslim - 3%.

However, caste-wise distribution of the population in Tendua Hiran Kuddi is as mentioned here: -

(i) Scheduled Castes - 18%.

(ii) Other Backward Castes - 26%.

(iii) General Category Castes - 56%.

The collective village level information of the four select villages in district Unnao is as follows: -

Table 3.4. Demographic Profiles of Selected Villages in District Unnao

Villages → *Particulars↓*	*Vill.: Mehndi-khera Block: Hasanganj*	*Vill.: Hasanganj Block: Hasanganj*	*Vill.: Khajuri Block: Nawabganj*	*Vill.: Tendua Hiran Kuddi Block: Nawabganj*
Total Households	387	660	37	332
S.C. Households	144 (37%)	112 (17%)	21 (57%)	56 (17%)
O.B.C. Households	135 (35%)	213 (32%)	Nil	98 (30%)
General Households	96 (25%)	310 (47%)	16 (43%)	158 (49%)
Muslim Households	12 (3%)	25 (4%)	Nil	10 (3%)
No. of BPL Households	176 (46%)	225 (34%)	12 (32%)	156 (48%)
Total Population	1956	4200	184	1782
Female	902	1958	93	862
Male	1054	2242	91	920
S. C.	1075 (55%)	984 (24%)	128 (70%)	320 (18%)
O. B. C.	566 (29%)	1526 (36%)	Nil	462 (26%)
General	315 (16%)	1690 (40%)	56 (30%)	1000 (56%)

Source : Village Development Officers of respective villages.

Note: SC means Scheduled Caste, OBC is Other Backward Caste and BPL is Below Poverty Line. Figures in brackets denote the percentage. NA denotes Data Not Available.

The proportion of the rural households below

poverty line is as high as 60 to 74 per cent in Sitapur, Shravasti, Raebareli, Unnao, Ambedkar Nagar, Sonbhadra, Hamirpur, Mirzapur, Bahraich, Kaushambi, Hardoi and as low as approximately 9% in Ghaziabad, Meerut and Baghpat districts of the state.

The foregoing description of socio-economic and demographic profiles of the study area - state, sample districts and sample villages provide us basic understanding of the study area. The socio-economic and demographic profiles indicate that the selected villages have considerable population living below poverty line. Hence, the need and scope of NREGS implementation until the people are alleviated from the clutches of poverty. The employment guarantee scheme rightly intends to address the backwardness by generating employment opportunities and thereby removing poverty and social inequality as per policy prescription. Against this backdrop, the next Chapter attempts to analyse the performance and progress of NREGS in the state. While our central focus is on the State of U.P., we also try to provide comparative analysis with all-India and also with some major States.

REFERENCES

1 Government of Utter Pradesh (2007), Human Development Report 2003: Uttar Pradesh, State Planning Commission, U.P. Yojana Bhawan, Lucknow.

2 World Bank, (2002) India: Confronting Poverty: The Challenge of Uttar Pradesh (Draft). PREM: South Asia Region.

4
NREGS : Performance in Uttar Pradesh Macro Level Analysis

The National Rural Employment Guarantee Act 2005 (NREGA) is being implemented in the state of Uttar Pradesh as per a notification Rural Development of the state Government – Vide Section 7 of the NREGA No. 107/38-7-2006-8 NREGA dated February 8, 2007. The Uttar Pradesh Rural Employment Guarantee Scheme (UPREGS) covers 22 most backward districts in the first phase of its implementation. These are Azamgarh, Banda, Barabanki, Chandauli, Chitrakoot, Fatehpur, Gorakhpur, Hamirpur, Hardoi, Jalaum, Jaunpur, Kaushambi, Kheri, Kushinagar, Lalitpur, Mahoba, Mirzapur, Pratapgarh, Raebareli, Sitapuri, Sonebhadra and Unnao. These 22 districts constitute about 11% of total 200 identified backward districts all over the country in the first phase of the NREGA implementation.

The UPREGS (NREGA) is to enhance livelihood security in rural areas by providing at least 100 days of guaranteed wage employment. Under this scheme rural households have a right to register themselves with the local Gram Panchayats, and seek employment under the Act. Work is to be provided within 15 days of the date of demand, failing which the State Government will have to pay unemployment allowance at the stipulated rates. This work guarantee can also serve other objectives such as generating productive assets, protecting the environment, empowering rural women, reducing rural-urban migration and fostering social equity. The innovative part of this programme is creation of job card and engagement of labourers in work on demand. Job Card entitles the card holder the right to work and payment thereon.

NREGS: PERFORMANCE AT A GLANCE

The analysis mainly focuses on the first phase of the NREGS implementation and based on the secondary data available at district level for the period of 2006-07. The secondary data relating to different aspects of NREGS performance has been analysed under the four major aspects.

1. demand for work and extent to which work have been met;
2. employment generated (in term of person days);
3. number of works completed and creation of community assets; and
4. pattern of fund utilization and wage payments.

The broad contours of the NREGS in UP for the year 2006-07 are given in Box No. 4.1

A close look at box 4.1 reveals a satisfactorily progress of the scheme. However, women participation is very low, material cost on higher side and average day of employment is one-fifth of the specified days i.e. 22 days against 100 days.

1. Demand for Work

Box 4.1: Status of NREGS in Uttar Pradesh - 2006-07

NREGS Implementation		**Employment Generation**	
⇒ No. of Districts:	22	⇒ No. of man-days generated (lakhs)	822.91
		Share of SCs	57%
⇒ Gram Panchayats:	18247	STs	3%
		Non-SC/ST	40%
⇒ No. of households demand employment (lakhs)	26.76	Women	17%
		⇒ Average days of employment:	22
⇒ No. of households received employment (lakhs)	25.73	⇒ Proportion of households received 100days of employment	6%
Work		**Fund utilization**	
⇒ No. works undertaken	84769	⇒ Proportion of expenditure against total available fund	75%
⇒ No. works completed	55389	On Wage	59%
		Material	35%

Source: NREGA Web Portal: http://nrega.nic.in (NREGA Implementation Status Report Part-I for Uttar Pradesh, Ministry of Rural Development, GoI)

The main objective of NREGA is to meet employment demand. The Jobs demanded by the unskilled household workers and the job provided under the scheme in different states are depicted in Figure 4.1. It reveals that in Uttar Pradesh, the households demanding employment stands at 26.76 lakhs and households were provided employment stands at 25.73 lakhs during the first phase of NREGS implementation (2006-07).

Further, Figure 4.1 reveals that the job demanded and job provided under the scheme have been met in all most all states. The main objective of NREGA, therefore have been achieved. The number of households demanding employment at national level is 2.12 cores. households and about 99 per cent of households (2.10 crore) have received work per the available data. The other states such as Andhra Pradesh, Rajsthan and Jharkhand have provided work to all the households (100%), which demanded the work opportunities as against 96.15% in Uttar Pradesh on this count.

Fig. 4.1. Status of Demand for Employment (2006-07)

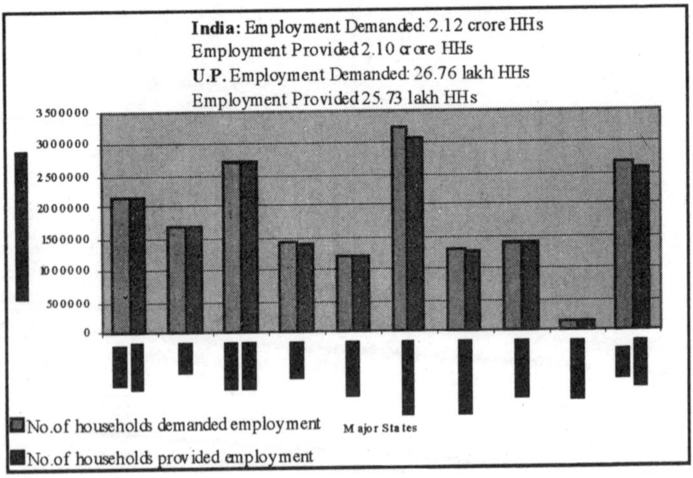

Source: Status Report, National Rural Employment Guarantee Act 2005 (NREGA), NREGA Web Portal (http://nrega.nic.in) Ministry of Rural Development, Government of India

2. Employment Generation

Under the employment guarantee scheme, it is required to identify various jobs in the identified districts of the State. The employment opportunities need to be created in the works related to water conservation and water harvesting, drought proofing, flood control, renovation of traditional water bodies, land development and rural connectivity. By and large, the jobs demanded by the major social groups include Scheduled Castes and Tribes, landless labourers and Other Backward Classes.

The beneficiaries of job creation (mandays) in different states are presented in Figure 4.2.

Fig. 4.2. Major Share of Households in Employment Generation

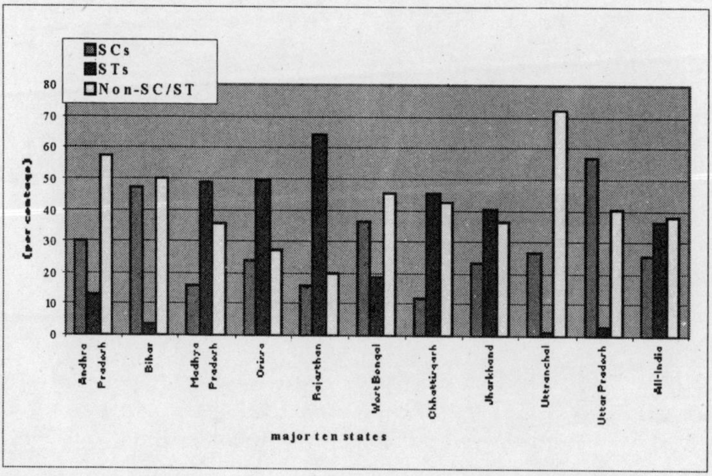

Source: Status Report, National Rural Employment Guarantee Act 2005 (NREGA), NREGA Web Portal (http://nrega.nic.in) Ministry of Rural Development, Government of India

As regards the major share of employment generated by various works is concerned, the available data reveals that more than half of households belong to Scheduled Castes (SCs), forming 56.85 per cent in the state. The share of other community (Non-SCs/STs) and by the Tribes (Scheduled Tribes) has been 40.04% and 3.11% respectively.

WOMEN PARTICIPATION IN NREGS

The Act stipulates that priority shall be given to

women so that 1/3rd of the beneficiaries are women who have registered and requested for work under the scheme.

Fig. 4.3. Share of Women in Employment under NREGS (2006-07)

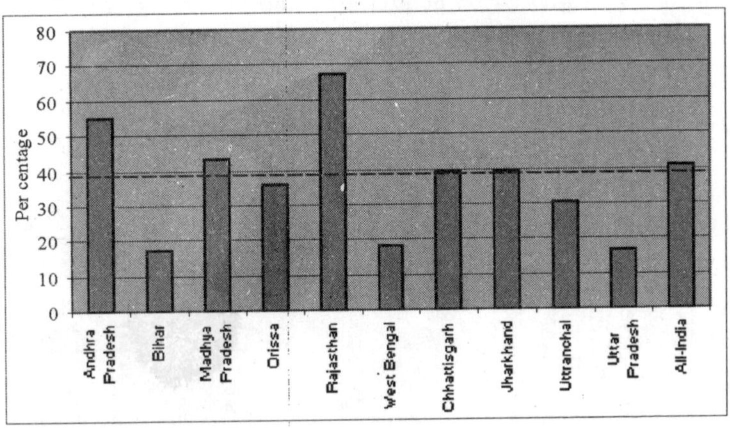

Source: Status Report, National Rural Employment Guarantee Act 2005 (NREGA), NREGA Web Portal (http://nrega.nic.in) Ministry of Rural Development, Government of India

Women participation as indicated by figure 4.3 is highest in Rajasthan and Andhra Pradesh which is higher than the national average at 41.6 per cent. However, in Uttar Pradesh women participation is only 17 percent.

The possible reasons for such a shortfall in women participation may be on account of the well entrenched tradition in the society, Pardha system particularly in the Northern states, and the lack of child care. This situation is still worse in U.P. where the jobs provided to the women stand is only 17% as against the stipulated rate of 33% and as well as lower than the national average which is relatively higher at 41 per cent.

Another important objective of NREGA is to provide 100 days of employment for rural households. It is evident that only 6% households out of total households demanded work have received 100 days of employment in the state of U.P. as indicated in Figure 4.4.

Fig. 4.4. Percentage Households who received 100 days employment

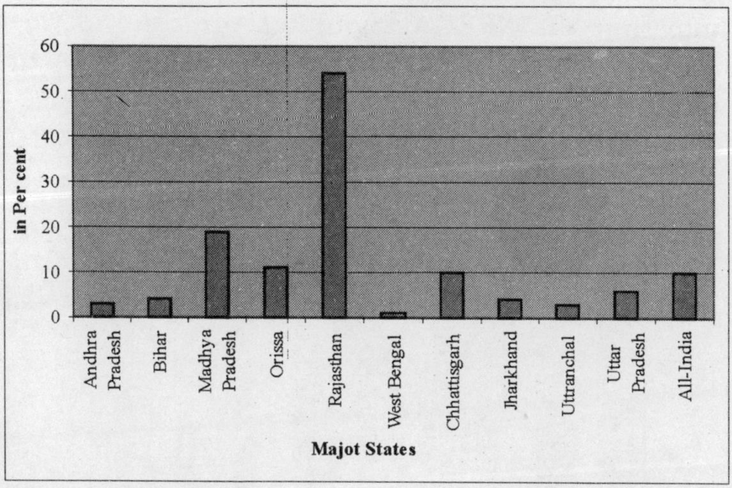

Source: Government of India, National Rural Employment Guarantee Act 2005 (NREGA) Report of the Second Year, April 2006-March 2007, Department of Rural Development, Ministry of Rural Development, New Delhi. 2008

However, the achievement at the national level in this regard has been 10%. The only state was Rajasthan spectacularly performed in providing 100 days of employment to the more than half of the households (54%) against the total households received employment. While the state of West Bengal simmers at shear 1% on this parameter.

3. Fund Utilization Pattern

Another important aspect of NREGS progress can be viewed from the fund utilization pattern by various states. The Government of India has established a fund called National Employment Guarantee Fund, from which the grants are released directly to the districts. Revolving funds are to be set up under NREGS at the District, Block and Gram Panchayat levels, with separate bank accounts being opened for such funds at each level. It is worth to note that the NREGA stipulates the ratio of wage cost to material costs should be no less than the minimum norm of 60:40.

Fig. 4.5. Fund Utilization Patterns of NREGS (2006-07)

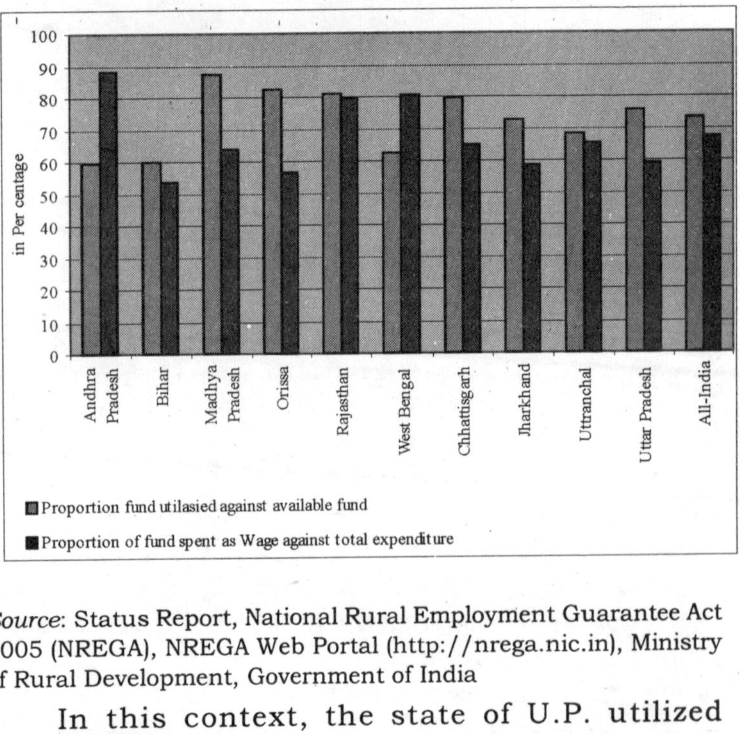

Source: Status Report, National Rural Employment Guarantee Act 2005 (NREGA), NREGA Web Portal (http://nrega.nic.in), Ministry of Rural Development, Government of India

In this context, the state of U.P. utilized considerable portions of the available fund, the proportion of amount spent is higher (75%) than the national average (73.08%). But few other states like Madhya Pradesh, Rajasthan, and Chhattisgarh have utilized the fund in greater proportion than that of U.P.

4. Creating Community Assets

Creating community assets is an important objective of the NREGA. The operational guideline issued by the Ministry of Rural Development, Government of India accords high priority to creating community assets. As per Schedule 1 of the Act, the focus of the NREGS in employment generation through creation of community assets shall be on the following works:

* Water conservation and water harvesting
* Drought proofing, including afforestation and tree plantation
* Irrigation canals, including micro and minor irrigation works
* Provision of irrigation facility to land owned by household belonging to the SC/ST, or to land of the beneficiaries of land reforms, or to land of the beneficiaries under the Indira Awas Yojana
* Renovation of traditional water bodies, including de-silting of tanks; Land development
* Flood control and protection works, including drainage in waterlogged areas
* Rural connectivity to provide all weather access. The construction of roads may include culverts where necessary, and within the village area may be taken up along with drains
* Any work that may be notified by the Central

Government in consultation with the State Government.

In terms of implementation priority, the NREGA operational guideline mandates that maximum emphasis should be on water conservation. Against this backdrop, the Figure 4.6 indicates the details of work undertaken during the first phase of NREGA implementation for the financial year 2006-07. The detail given in the Figure 4.6 clearly shows that the measures of various community assets created under the NREGS in the state during the period 2006-07. It appears that the rural connectivity related assets have received the precedence over all other type of assets in the state of U.P.

Fig. 4.6. Assets Created Under NREGS in U.P., 2006-07

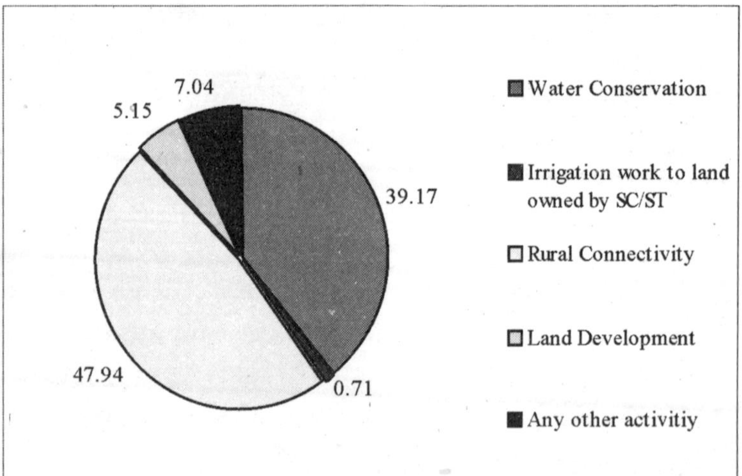

Source: Government of India, (2008) National Rural Employment Guarantee Act 2005 (NREGA) Report of the Second Year, April 2006-March 2007, Department of Rural Development, Ministry of Rural Development, New Delhi.

It is notable from the figure 4.6 that about 48

percent of the assets were in form of rural connectivity followed by 39 percent of assets in the area of water conservation. The works related to the land development could be accomplished up to 5 per cent and the irrigation work on the land owned by the SCs/STs has been 0.7%. only in the entire gamut of the assets creation. It may also be noted that the participation of SCs in NREGS even though larger portion (57 %), the assets creation in term of creating irrigation facilities to land owned by the SCs show the negligence. This kind of anomaly also merits thoughtful and in-depth investigation by scholars.

NREGS PERFORMANCE IN SELECTED FOUR DISTRICTS

As per as the availability of fund is concerned, the state had Rs.102871.223 lakh for carrying out NREGS activities, out of this the state spent Rs.77967.464 lakh, i.e. 75 percent of total available fund during the financial year 2006-07. The works, which have been undertaken in the state to create durable assets, are mainly rural connectivity, water conservation and water harvesting, renovation of traditional water bodies (tanks/ponds, canals, open wells, etc). There was about 84769 works undertaken and out of this 55389, i.e. 65 percent of work completed (nrega.nic.in). The detail presentation of districts and block level data related to NREGS performance as follows:

1. Barabanki District

As the NREGS Report of Barabanki dated 8 – 12 – 2006 shows that the total fund availability stands Rs. 5175.36 lakhs. Out of this, a sum of Rs. 3539.34 lakhs, i.e. 68.39%, has been spent towards the implementation of the scheme. Further, the number of applications received for registration was 326521 and there were 326314 households registered. It is a matter of great satisfaction that the job cards distribution has been 100%. Besides this, as many as 110510 labourers to whom employment was provided, 62.29% were from among the Scheduled Castes while the participation of women stood at 1.30% only. The extent of employment demanded was for 3846320 man-days but the total number of man days generated were 3685215, i.e. an achievement of 95.81%.

It may also be mentioned that the contribution of scheduled castes in the total man days generated has been 64.82% (in absolute terms 2388840 mandays). Contribution of women in this stands just at 0.08%. It is also laudable that all the labourers demanding work, i.e. 110510, got the employment opportunities. There were 68841 labourers, i.e. 62.3%, from among scheduled castes and the number of women, being 1442, remained restricted to 1.30%. All told, out of registered households, i.e. 326314, the employment opportunities could be availed of by 94119 households only, i.e. 28.84%. Lastly, 934 projects have been completed and 4374 projects of various kinds have been started under the NREGA scheme in the district (See Annexure 4).

Banki Block

There are 62 Gram Panchayats having 14718 BPL households according to the Block's report dated 9 – 12 – 2006. The number of verified and registered applications for working in the scheme stands 16480. It means that as many as 1760 applicant households from above poverty line have also been included. However, the job cards issued were 16465 including 17117 members from the registered households. While the number of households demanding work stood at 2258, the number of members from these households demanding work was 2470 in order to generate 47668 man days. In this figure woman's contribution was only 93 days. It may also be mentioned that out of 47668 man days generated, 60% man days were contributed by scheduled caste people while 35% by others and less than 1% by women. Further, out of 2452 workers to whom work was provided, 70% were from scheduled castes and 30% belonged to other castes. In this block 139 works have been started at Gram Panchayat level under NREGA scheme indicating 78.30% expenditure from the available funds since 1.4.2006. It needs to be probed, however, why only 13.71% households out of registered and job card holding households demanded work. (See Annexure 5).

Dewa Block

There are 76 Gram Panchayats having 13423 BPL households as shown in the Block's report dated 10 – 12 – 2006. The number of verified and registered applications for working in the scheme stands 16845. All these households were issued job cards and have 16945 members eligible to work under the scheme. The number of works started at Gram Panchayat level in Dewa block is 96. Further, the number of households demanding work being 2805 indicates that only 16.65% out of 16845 households have shown interest to find work. It may be noted here that 3422 households outside BPL category aspired to work under the scheme. The data shows that out of 2805 households demanding work, 2795 households were provided work. Thus, in this sense the achievement has been 99.64% to generate 34778 man days. The extent of contribution of scheduled castes workers in generating these many man days is 69.32%. Moreover, out of 2840 members demanding work, 2822, i.e. 99.30%, were provided work. Again, out of 2822 workers, 1959, i.e. 69.41%, workers were from scheduled castes. The participation of women in the work was negligible as only 4 women preferred to work under the scheme. Lastly, only 38.38% of total funds could be utilized since 1 – 4 – 2006 in this block (See Annexure 6).

2. Raebareli District

According to the available data in the Progress Report upto 07 – 02 – 07, in other words, the performance of the scheme one year after its, launching on Feb. 2, 2006; as many as 366649 applications were received for registration from all the 21 blocks of the district. Out of this 342365 households could be registered by this time. 326176 Job Cards were distributed to the registered households but the number of applications for demanding the work stood only 185544, i.e. 56.88%, of the total distributed job cards. The total demand for work amounted to generation of 3856265 person days. However, 3724431 person days were generated, i.e. 96.58%. Out of these, 37.24 lakh person days, 20.86 lakh person days, i.e. 56%, were generated by the households belonging to scheduled castes. However, the share of women in this regard was only 7.16 lakhs, i.e. 19.22%.

Now coming to the number of workers who were provided work in the district, 1.70 lakh people received the benefit of working under the scheme and out of this, 1.02 lakh workers belonged to the scheduled caste, i.e. 60%. It is a matter of satisfaction that the share of women participation was found 30%. Further, the share of households having got the job in the number of registered household was 48%. It may also be mentioned that 3526 activities were started ever since the introduction of NREGA and the district accomplished 4080 different kinds of works. In one year, 68.13% of funds were utilized in Raebareli. There are 21 blocks in the district (See Annexure 7).

Shivagarh Block

In Shivagarh block, 88% of funds were spent by 22 – 1 – 2007. The block received 13667 applications for registration. It is satisfying to observe that 13234 households were registered and all of them received the job card. But only 55.56% of the households demanded the work. This was equivalent to generation of 1.34 lakh person days. Eventually, the block succeeded in achieving almost 100% result as far as generation of person days, is concerned. The participation of scheduled castes in the generation of person days of work was 60%. However, the share of women in this respect was woefully low, i.e. 2.14%.

As regards, the workers who were provided job, out of 7354 applicants all received the employment with a share of 62% of the workers from scheduled castes. Again, it is a cause of concern that only 4.4% women were employed in Shivagarh block during one year approximately after the introduction of the scheme. Lastly, 7118 households were provided employment out of 13234 registered households, i.e. 58%, and as many as 339 works were completed in the block. There was 39 Gram Panchayat in Shivagarh block (See Annexure 8).

Bachharawan Block

Exactly within one year of the promulgation of the scheme, i.e. by Feb. 3, 2007, the block was able to spend 81% of the amount from the amount available. The block received 20131 applications for registration, and 18442 households were registered. However, 15163 job cards could be distributed and out of this only 8314, i.e. 55%, applications were received for demanding the work to generate 1.57 lakh of person days. The share of scheduled castes in generating person days stood about 60% but the contribution of women in this regard was only 16.34% while 8314 applicants demanded the work; it was not possible to provide work to all of them. Only 7916 households were provided employment. It is worth to mention that the block completed 165 types work in the entire block. There are 46 Gram Panchayats in Bachharawan block of Raebareli District (Annexure 9).

3. Sitapur District

There are 19 blocks in the district of Sitapur. The NREGA Progress Report dated 12 - 2 - 2007 shows that by this time 313712 job cards were distributed in the district. 2.02 lakh workers got the job under the scheme to generate 43.85 lakhs of person days. However, only 39.9 lakh of person days could be generated and the share of women in this regard was negligible, i.e. only 20863 person days. The share of employment of scheduled castes was 6.70% approximately while only 1.1% women workers participated in the scheme. Nearly 65% of available funds were utilized in the district in the implementation of National Rural Employment Guarantee Scheme in Sitapur(Annexure 10).

Sidhauli Block

There are 71 Gram Panchayats in Sidhauli block of Sitapur District. The block received a total of 11107 applications for registration. As the record sheet of the block shows, 6981 job cards were distributed among scheduled castes and 3659 job cards to the households of other categories. It may be mentioned that 4760 households demanded employment, and 4556 households, i.e. 96%, were provided the job. In the households which demanded the work, there were 5758 workers and 6469 workers were provided the job. (Annexure 11).

Gondalamau Block

There are 74 Gram Panchayats in this block, while 16798 applications were received for the registration under the scheme, 14978 job cards were distributed. The share of job cards distributed to scheduled castes was 68%. It may be mentioned that out of 5272 applicant households, the work was provided to 5241 households, i.e. to 99.41%. By 15 – 12 – 2006, 1.26 lakh person days were generated and the workers from scheduled castes contributed to the extent of 57%. Out of 10188 employed workers for doing the unskilled manual job, there were 5984 workers, i.e. 59%, from scheduled castes. It is again a matter of serious concern that the number of women employed in the scheme was merely 130, which shows a negligible degree of participation. (See Annexure 12).

4. Unnao District

There are 16 blocks in the district having 2.83 lakhs population living below the poverty line. The Progress Report upto 31 – 1 – 2007, shows that the district received 2.05 lakhs applications for registration under the scheme. All these applications were verified

Box 4.2. Number of Households received 100 days of Employment

	Block	No. of Households
1.	Asoha	15
2.	Bichhia	105
3.	Bighapur	21
4.	Miyanganj	5
5.	Purarva	67
6.	Safipur	85
	Total	298

Source: District Rural Development Agency, Unnao

and the job cards were distributed to 2.03 lakh, i.e. 99%, households out of 112691 total workers who were provided work, there are 67901, i.e. 60% workers from scheduled castes. The share of women participation in the NREGA works was miserably low, i.e. 0.01%. The data shows that 298 households from six blocks got 100 days of employment as detailed hereunder:- (also see Annexure 13).

Nawabganj Block

There are 72 Gram Panchayats in this block. The Progress Report upto 07 – 02 – 2007 does not provide detailed information. However, it mentions that 13532 job cards were distributed in this block although 14327 households were registered. Notwithstanding the lack of relevant information related to seven Gram Panchayats, it appears that the block was able to generate 2.21 lakh person days. (See Annexure 14).

Hasanganj Block

There are 70 Gram Panchayats in Hasanganj block of Unnao district. The Progress Sheet upto 18 –

2 – 2007 shows that 9397 applications were received for registration. However, after the required exercise of verification, 9551 households were registered and as many as 9260, i.e. 97%, job cards were distributed. There were 4693 applications for demand of work and the same numbers of workers were provided the job, generating 1.62 lakh person days. The block was able to utilize 78% of the available amount in carrying out various activities under the scheme. (See Annexure 15).

The survey results show that the majority of beneficiary workers in the age group of 18-35 years old. The majority of workers who sought job under the NREGS in almost all the villages surveyed were from scheduled caste (SCs) and other backward castes. The finding reveals that beneficiaries came from SC households as casual labour in agriculture and as landless population. Further, the socio-economic profiles of beneficiaries show the objectives and benefits of the NREGA reaching to the target group.

The respondents in all the districts came to know about the work opportunity through village Panchayats.The Gram Sabha provided necessary help to the villagers to inform correct information at right time about the NREGA. As we found from our survey that the Gram Sabha played major role in assisting villagers willing to work 100% in Barabanki one of our study area. It appears that the respondents in the study villages got the opportunity to work relatively longer period in a month (10-20 days).

The above analysis provides us the performance and progress of NREGS in the state of Uttar Pradesh. The analysis focused at state and four selected district level of NREGS first phase implantation (2006-07). As per the NREGA guidelines and available data relating to the different aspects of NREGS performance and progress, the analysis broadly focuses on four major aspects. Such as demand for work and extent to which work have been met; employment generated (in term of person days); number of works completed and creation of community assets; and pattern of fund utilization and wage payments. An overall analysis show that a satisfactorily progress of the scheme. However, women participation is very low, material cost on higher side and average day of employment is one-fifth of the specified days, i.e. 22 days against 100 days.

The main objective of NREGA is to meet employment demands. The jobs demanded by the unskilled household workers and the job provided under the scheme in Uttar Pradesh, reveals that about 25.73 lakhs and households were provided employment as agsisnt to 26.76 lakhs demand jobs. In case of employment generated by various works is concerned, the available data reveals that more than half of households belong to Scheduled Castes (SCs) forming 56.85 per cent in the state. The share of other community (Non-SCs/STs) and by the Tribes (Scheduled Tribes) has been 40.04% and 3.11% respectively. While the participation of SCs has been more than double of the national average (25.35%), the share of women in employment under NREGS in the state has been far below the national average. However, participation of women in the scheme in NREGS is less than the stipulated requirement (33 per cent) as stand at only 17 percent.

Another important aspect of NREGS progress can be viewed from the fund utilization pattern. The state of U.P. utilized considerable portion of available fund, the proportion of amount spent is higher (75%) than the national average (73.08%), but few other states like Madhya Pradesh, Rajasthan, and Chhattisgarh have utilized the fund in greater proportion than that of U.P. Similar observation has been found at the district level as well.

Creating community assets are another aspect of NREGA objectives. In U.P. it appears that the rural connectivity related assets have received the precedence over all other type of assets in the state of U.P. The works related to the land development could be accomplished up to 5 per cent and the irrigation work on the land owned by the SCs/STs has been 0.7%. only in the entire gamut of the assets creation. It may also be noted that the participation of SCs in NREGS even though larger portion (57 %), the assets creation in term of creating irrigation facilities to land owned by the SCs show the negligence. Lastly, it is evident that only 6% households out of total households demanded work have received 100 days of employment in the state of U.P. However, the achievement at the national level in this regard has been 10%. The only state was Rajasthan spectacularly performed in providing 100 days of employment to the more than half of the households (54%) against the total households received employment.

5

NREGS :

Performance at Village Level

Survey Analysis and Interpretation of Beneficiaries Responses

This research study was conducted in four districts, eight blocks and sixteen villages in the state of Uttar Pradesh. A detailed questionnaire was administrated on four hundred beneficiaries at different work sites in sixteen villages. The data colleted from the beneficiaries and other functionaries associated with the scheme are analysed and interpreted below.

AGE OF RESPONDENTS

The Table 5.1 shows that the beneficiary workers in the age group of 18-35 years were 81%, in Barabanki, followed by Raebareli (65%), Unnao (65%) and Sitapur 59%. Thus, out of the total sample 67.50% workers belonged to this age group. While 25% workers in all the districts were from 36-45 age groups, only 1% was above 55 years.

AGE OF MEMBERS IN THE RESPONDENT HOUSE HOLDS

Table 5.2 indicates age-wise distribution in respondent household — District-wise.

It is evident from the data, that 60% of the members were dependent in Sitapur thus leaving only

Table 5.1 : Age of Respondents

	Sitapur	Raebareli	Unnao	Barabanki	Total
Less than 18 years	0	0	0	0	0
%	0.00	0.00	0.00	0.00	0.00
18 - 35 years	59	65	65	81	270
%	59.00	65.00	65.00	81.00	67.50
36 - 45 years	36	26	24	14	100
%	36.00	26.00	24.00	14.00	25.00
46 - 55 years	4	7	11	4	26
%	4.00	7.00	11.00	4.00	6.50
Above 55 years	1	2	0	1	4
%	1.00	2.00	0.00	1.00	1.00
N	100	100	100	100	400

Source: Computed from filled in Questionnaires

Table 5.2. Age-wise Distribution of Members in the Respondents' households.

Age Group	Sitapur	Raebareli	Unnao	Barabanki	Total
Below 18 years	224	255	228	128	835
%	52.96	52.47	46.72	61.84	52.06
19 - 25 years	52	51	62	33	198
%	12.29	10.49	12.70	15.94	12.34
26 - 35 years	55	66	64	18	203
%	13.00	13.58	13.11	8.70	12.66
36 - 45 years	37	38	47	6	128
%	8.75	7.82	9.63	2.90	7.98
46 - 55 years	27	30	56	10	123
%	6.38	6.17	11.48	4.83	7.67
Above 56 years	28	46	31	12	117
%	6.62	9.47	6.35	5.80	7.29
N	423	486	488	207	1604

Source: Computed from filled in Questionnaires

40% as working population. Raebarali has 62% dependent persons and 38% working members in the households of the respondents. In Unnao 53% are dependent and 47% working while in Barabanki 67% were found dependent members and only 33% in working age-group. Thus out of our total sample of 400 beneficiaries 59% were dependent members and 41% in working age group, requiring job opportunities.

BENEFICIARIES AMONG SOCIAL GROUPS

The majority of workers who sought job under the NREGS in almost all the villages surveyed were from scheduled caste (SCs) and other backward castes. As the Figure 5.1 shows that the highest number of respondents belonging to SCs was in Raebareli 76%, followed by Unnao (65%). The least were engaged in work in Barabanki (48%). But the percentage of other backward caste stands high in Barabanki (50%).

Thus, in sum total of the sample 61% were SC., 37% OBC and only 2% from General category. The finding reveals that beneficiaries came from SCs households as casual labour in agriculture and as landless population. Further, the socio-economic profiles of beneficiaries show the objectives and benefits of the NREGS are reaching to the target groups.

Fig. 5.1. Caste Structure of Respondents

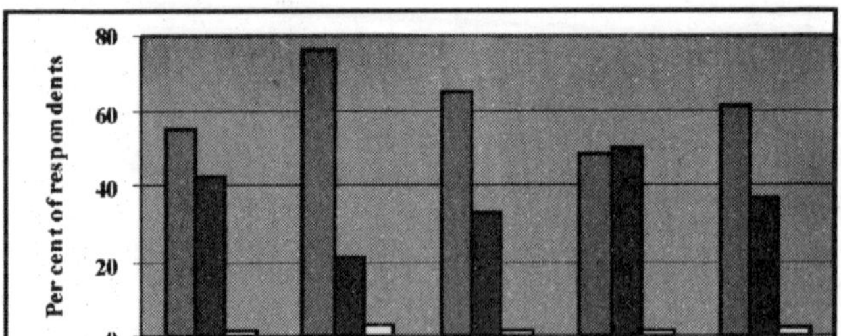

	Sitapur	Raebareli	Unnao	Barabanki	Total
SC	55	76	65	48	61
OBC	43	21	33	50	36.75
General	2	3	2	2	2.25

Source: Computed from filled in Questionnaires

SOURCE OF INFORMATION ABOUT THE SCHEME

The Table 5.3 reveals various sources of information about the NREGS to the villagers. It is significant to observe from the above Table 5.3 that role of Panchayati Raj Institutions (PRIs) i.e. village Panchayat has been vital because the maximum number (90%) of the respondents in all the districts came to know about the work opportunity through village Panchayats. While the rest of them got the information through rally in the village, block level notice board, etc.

Table 5.3. Source of Information about NREGS

Source of Information	*Sitapur*	*Raebareli*	*Unnao*	*Barabanki*	*Total*
Rally	4	0	4	0	8
%	4.00	0.00	4.00	0.00	2.00
Visit	1	0	2	0	3
%	1.00	0.00	2.00	0.00	0.75
Village	1	1	2	2	6
%	1.00	1.00	2.00	2.00	1.50
Village Panchayat	94	99	91	77	361
%	94.00	99.00	91.00	77.00	90.25
Block Level Notice Board	0	0	1	21	22
%	0.00	0.00	1.00	21.00	5.50
District Level Notice Board	0	0	0	0	0
%	0.00	0.00	0.00	0.00	0.00
N	100	100	100	100	400

Source: Computed from filled in Questionnaires

ROLE OF GRAM SABHA

The Gram Sabha provides necessary help to the villagers correct information at right time about the

NREGS. We found from our survey that the Gram Sabha played major role in assisting villagers who were willing to work. 100% in Barabanki; 97% in Raebareli; 80%, Sitapur and 78% in Unnao. In sum, out of the total sample of 400, in 89% cases the Gram Sabha helped the people in the registration of the beneficiaries. Table 5.4 shows the extent of assistance provided to the villagers in the process of their registration under the scheme.

Table 5.4. Role of Gram Sabha

	Sitapur	*Raebareli*	*Unnao*	*Barabanki*	*Total*
Yes	80	97	78	100	355
%	80.00	97.00	78.00	100.00	88.75
No	20	3	22	0	45
%	20.00	3.00	22.00	0.00	11.25
N	100	100	100	100	400

Source: Computed from filled in Questionnaires

SOURCE OF INFORMATION ABOUT EMPLOYMENT

Generally, there are various sources through which the registered persons come to know about their employment in the villages. Table 5.5 contains various sources.

Table 5.5 shows that 54% of workers got the information about their employment through the members of the village level committee, 27% from the village Panchayat, 16% from notice board of Panchayat office and 3% from the BDOs acting as the Programme Officers.

DURATION OF WORK AT SITE

Table 5.6 shows the range of days when the respondents were engaged in works at various

Table 5.6. Number of Working Days

Days	*Sitapur*	*Raebareli*	*Unnao*	*Barabanki*	*Total*
1 -10	22	2	34	8	66
%	22.00	2.00	34.00	8.00	16.50
11 – 20	30	16	30	22	98
%	30.00	16.00	30.00	22.00	24.50
21 – 30	32	78	23	57	190
%	32.00	78.00	23.00	57.00	47.50
More than 30	16	4	13	13	46
%	16.00	4.00	13.00	13.00	11.50
N	100	100	100	100	400

Source: Computed from filled in Questionnaires

worksites in the different villages.

It appears from the Table 5.6 that 34% of the respondents in Unnao, 22% in Sitapur, 8% in Barabanki and 2% in Raebreli got the opportunity to work from 1 to 10 days. Those who worked from 11 to 20 days, they were 30% in both the district i.e. Sitapur and Unnao. It was only in Raebareli that only 16% worked from 11 to 20 days. Further, the respondents who worked from 21 to 30 days were maximum in Raebareli, followed by Barabanki (57%), Sitapur (32%) and 23% in Unnao. Thus, out of total sample, 48% of respondents worked between 21 to 30 days, 25% between 11 to 20 days 16.50% from 1 to 10 days and only 11.50% for more than 30 days. It stands clear that only 4% of respondents worked more than 30 days in Raebareli while the figures in Sitapur, Unnao and Barabanki are 16%, 13% and 13% respectively. There is need to provide employment of more working days at work sites.

Table 5.5. Information about Employment

	Sitapur	*Raebareli*	*Unnao*	*Barabanki*	*Total*
Letter from Village Panchayat	8	29	28	42	107
%	8.00	29.00	28.00	42.00	26.75
Letter from Programme Officer	4	0	2	5	11
%	4.00	0.00	2.00	5.00	2.75
Notice board of village panchayat office	26	14	21	1	62
%	26.00	14.00	21.00	1.00	15.50
Notice board of Programme Officer	0	0	1	2	3
%	0.00	0.00	1.00	2.00	0.75
Members of village level committee	62	57	48	50	217
%	62.00	57.00	48.00	50.00	54.25
N	100	100	100	100	400

Source: Computed from filled in Questionnaires

PARTICIPATION OF REGISTERED HOUSEHOLD MEMBERS IN THE SCHEME

While noting the responses from the villagers at the worksites regarding the participation of other members of their households, the following matrix comes to surface.

The Table 5.7 indicates about the number of family members who got employment in this scheme, 91 respondents in Sitapur told that only one member from his household is employed in this scheme. As far as other districts are concerned, 89 respondents in Barabanki, 84 in Unnao and 74 respondents in Raebareli had only one member of their family as the beneficiary of the scheme. In Raebareli 6 workers responded that there were three beneficiaries from their

Table 5.7. Participation of Household Members in the Scheme

	Sitapur	*Raebareli*	*Unnao*	*Barabanki*	*Total*
One	91	74	84	89	338
%	91.00	74.00	84.00	89.00	84.50
Two	9	20	13	8	50
%	9.00	20.00	13.00	8.00	12.50
Three	0	6	1	3	10
%	0.00	6.00	1.00	3.00	2.50
Four	0	0	2	0	2
%	0.00	0.00	2.00	0.00	0.50
N	100	100	100	100	400

Source: Computed from filled in Questionnaires

families. In Unnao 2 workers told that four members of their families have got the work in NREGS so far. Thus, 84.50% out of total sample of 400 respondents had only one member from their families as beneficiary of this scheme.

MINIMUM WAGES

The beneficiaries of the scheme are receiving the wages amounting the Rs.58/- as per Minimum Wages Act, 1948 which as applicable in U.P. since August 1st 2004. Indeed it is a matter of satisfaction that there is no under -payment of the wages to the workers as evident from the Table 5.8.

Table 5.8. Minimum Wages

Rupees	*Sitapur*	*Raebareli*	*Unnao*	*Barabanki*	*Total*
Rs. 58	100	100	100	100	400
%	100.00	100.00	100.00	100.00	100.00
N	100	100	100	100	400

Source: Computed from filled in Questionnaires

PAYMENT OF WAGES

While administering the interview schedule on the beneficiaries of the scheme at various work sites it was found that they receive their wages within prescribed time limit. The Table 5.9 shows that 99% respondents in Barabanki, 94% of them in Raebareli, 75% in Sitapur and 67% in Unnao received their wages on weekly basis. While 33% in Unnao, 25% in Sitapur, 6% in Raebareli and 1% in Barabanki received the wages within 15 days.

Table 5.9. Wage Payment Period

Duration	*Sitapur*	*Raebareli*	*Unnao*	*Barabanki*	*Total*
One Week	75	94	67	99	335
%	75.00	94.00	67.00	99.00	83.75
Two Weeks	25	6	33	1	65
%	25.00	6.00	33.00	1.00	16.25
More Than	0	0	0	0	0
%	0.00	0.00	0.00	0.00	0.00
N	100	100	100	100	400

Source: Computed from filled in Questionnaires

None of the respondents in all the four district told that the wage payment was delayed. It is great relief to learn that nearly 84% of the total sample beneficiaries got their wages in one week.

MODE OF PAYMENT OF WAGES

The survey team found that the workers did not receive their wages either through bank or post office in their areas. Table 5.10 indicates the mode of wage payments.

All the respondents in surveyed districts received their wages in cash on the Bazar days in their villages in the presence of people of the village community. When asked about the preference of receiving their

Table 5.10. Mode of Wage Payment

	Sitapur	*Raebareli*	*Unnao*	*Barabanki*	*Total*
Bank	0	0	0	0	0
%	0.00	0.00	0.00	0.00	0.00
Post Office	0	0	0	0	0
%	0.00	0.00	0.00	0.00	0.00
Cash	100	100	100	100	400
%	100.00	100.00	100.00	100.00	100.00
N	100	100	100	100	400

Source: Computed from filled in Questionnaires

wages through bank or Post Office they responded in negative.

DIFFICULTY IN GETTING WAGES

Normally there should not be any difficulty of paying wages to the workers but some how due to unforeseen situational context some of the workers did mention some difficulties.

Table 5.11. Problems in Wage Payment

	Sitapur	*Raebareli*	*Unnao*	*Barabanki*	*Total*
Yes	11	1	6	4	22
%	11.00	1.00	6.00	4.00	5.50
No	89	99	94	96	378
%	89.00	99.00	94.00	96.00	94.50
N	100	100	100	100	400

Source: Computed from filled in Questionnaires

It is indeed a cause of concern that a few workers faced some kind of difficulties in getting their wages. Although the share of such respondents in the total sample is merely 5.50% and rest of them had never faced any difficulty.

DISTANCE OF WORKING PLACE

As per norms of the scheme the worker should

get the employment within the radius of 5 kms of his/her residence. The survey depicts the following data in this regard.

Table 5.12. Distance of work site

	Sitapur	*Raebareli*	*Unnao*	*Barabanki*	*Total*
Within 5 Kilometers	99	100	100	100	399
%	99.00	100.00	100.00	100.00	99.75
More than 5 Kilometers	1	0	0	0	1
%	1.00	0.00	0.00	0.00	0.25
N	100	100	100	100	400

Source: Computed from filled in Questionnaires

In all the four districts the respondents told that their worksite is within 5km of their residences except only one respondent in Sitapur. In fact, he belonged to a village hamlet of the Gram Pancyayat called as 'majara' in vernacular which could be at little more than 5 kms.

WORK FACILITIES

The workers are entitled to a number of worksite facilities during their employment according to the provisions of the NREGS. Table 5.13 displays such facilities.

There was no arrangement of cre'che or balwadi since the women did not prefer to work in all the sample villages (worksites). As far as facilities of providing shade is concerned, it was shade of trees, Varandah of a nearby school, etc. Nothing sort of tent was found anywhere. Out of total sample, 43% workers reported to get some kind of shade while 57% of them candidly told that there were no such arrangements at the worksites.

Table 5.13. Work Site Facilities

	Sitapur	*Raebareli*	*Unnao*	*Barabanki*	*Total*
Creche	0	0	0	0	0
%	0.00	0.00	0.00	0.00	0.00
Shade	50	45	8	70	173
%	50.00	45.00	8.00	70.00	43.25
Balvadi	0	0	0	0	0
%	0.00	0.00	0.00	0.00	0.00
No Arrangement	50	55	92	30	227
%	50.00	55.00	92.00	30.00	56.75
N	100	100	100	100	400

Source: Computed from filled in Questionnaires

ARRANGEMENT OF DRINKING WATER

As regard the facility of drinking water at the worksites in all the districts the following data is revealed in the Table 5.14 hereunder :

Table 5.14. Availability of Drinking Water at site

	Sitapur	*Raebareli*	*Unnao*	*Barabanki*	*Total*
Yes	86	99	95	89	369
%	86.00	99.00	95.00	89.00	92.25
No	14	1	5	11	31
%	14.00	1.00	5.00	11.00	7.75
N	100	100	100	100	400

Source: Computed from filled in Questionnaires

The facility of drinking water to the workers in Raebareli was the best (99%), followed by Unnao (95%), Barabanki (89%) and Sitapur (86%). Out of total sample only 8% respondents reported that there was no proper arrangement of drinking water at the worksites.

ARRANGEMENT FIRST AID FACILITY AT THE WORKSITES

The NREGS has prescribed that there must be

First-Aid facility available at each worksite in order to treat any kind of injury caused to the workers while doing the manual work. The Table 5.15 presents the data from the survey at worksites.

Table 5.15. First-Aid Facilities at Work Site

	Sitapur	*Raebareli*	*Unnao*	*Barabanki*	*Total*
Yes	24	21	21	25	91
%	24.00	21.00	21.00	25.00	22.75
No	76	79	79	75	309
%	76.00	79.00	79.00	75.00	77.25
N	100	100	100	100	400

Source: Computed from filled in Questionnaires

Regarding the arrangement of first aid at the worksite only 23% of respondents told that there was some kind of bandage and cream or alum was available at the worksites, while 77% of them simply denied to have found any proper arrangement or a first-aid box.

FUTURE EMPLOYMENT OPPORTUNITY

The Survey team asked the labourers about their perspective as to the increase of job opportunities in their area. The data in this regard is presented in Table 5.16.

Table 5.16. Future Employment Opportunity

	Sitapur	*Raebareli*	*Unnao*	*Barabanki*	*Total*
Yes	99	100	95	93	387
%	99.00	100.00	95.00	93.00	96.75
No	1	0	5	7	13
%	1.00	0.00	5.00	7.00	3.25
N	100	100	100	100	400

Source: Computed from filled in Questionnaires

Considering the kind of works undertaken in all the four districts, like digging the ponds for water harvesting, cleaning of silt in the Nala (drain), cleaning of silt in the canals, laying the brick roads (Kharanja), making Kuchcha roads, plantation, etc. the 97% of total respondents were of the view that such works will help create job opportunities in the villages. The ponds may be used for fisheries, rearing Singhara (a vegetable). Kharanja roads will increase connectivity to other places and motivate the people to take up trading activities. Plantation also will be a durable asset in the villages. Only 3% respondents saw no possibility of increasing the job opportunities. However, there is need to link these activities to some trading, vocations, crafts, skills building by providing micro-finance.

FEELING HAPPY WITH THIS SCHEME

Whether the village people working under the scheme feel happy in getting the job in their areas, the responses are as shown in Table 5.17.

Table 5.17. Satisfaction with Job Opportunity

	Sitapur	*Raebareli*	*Unnao*	*Barabanki*	*Total*
Yes	96	99	94	100	389
%	96.00	99.00	94.00	100.00	97.25
No	4	1	6	0	11
%	4.00	1.00	6.00	0.00	2.75
N	100	100	100	100	400

Source: Computed from filled in Questionnaires

It is notable that 100% respondents in Barabanki, 99% in Raebareli, 96% in Sitapur and 94% in Unnao exuded happiness that they got an opportunity to do gainful work in and around their own place for the duration they wanted. Thus, they can look after their agricultural work as well as earn money in their own village under this scheme. Migration to city centres in distress for search of job was bound to be reduced.

SUMMARY REMARKS

The survey results show that the majority of beneficiary workers were in the age group of 18-35 years old. The majority of workers who sought job under the NREGS in almost all the villages surveyed were from scheduled caste (SCs) and other backward castes. The finding reveals that beneficiaries came from SCs households as casual labour in agriculture and as landless population. Further, the socio-economic profiles of beneficiaries show the objectives and benefits of the NREGS reaching to the target groups.

The respondents in all the districts came to know about the work opportunity through village Panchayats.The Gram Sabha provided necessary help to the villagers to inform correct information at right time about the NREGS. As we found from our survey that the Gram Sabha played major role in assisting villagers willing to work, 100% in Barabanki, one of our study area. It appears that the respondents in the study villages got the opportunity to work relatively longer period in a month (10-20 days).

The result indicates about the number of family members who got employment in this scheme, majority of respondents (91 per cent) in our study villages told that only one member from his household is employed in this scheme

The beneficiaries of the scheme are receiving the wages amounting the Rs.58/- as per Minimum Wages Act, 1948 which as applicable in U.P. since August 1st 2004. Indeed it is a matter of satisfaction that there is no under -payment of the wages to the workers as evident from the study.

We also found that they received their wages

within prescribed time limit-weekly basis. The survey team found that the workers in surveyed districts received their wages in cash on the Bazar days in their villages and do not receive their wages either through bank or post office in their areas. In case of peoples perception about the scheme, it was found that all most all respondents (100% in our study areas) exuded happiness that they got an opportunity to do gainful work in and around their own place of residences for the duration they want. Thus they can look after their agricultural work as well as earn money in their own village under this scheme. The study observed that the NREGS tend to address the issue of migration to city in distress for search of job and was bound to be reduced.

During our course of survey at village work sites we also found that particularly disabled person at one site was employed. At another site stones were being broken with iron *belchas* and at third site, as usual information board regarding various aspects of jobs was displayed. These pictures are shown on next pages.

A disabled person employed at the work site.

Vill. : Mehndikheda, Block : Hasanganj, District : Unnao

Job Card holders breaking a stone by iron *belchas* :
(Dr. S.K. Bajpai at the work site)
Vill. Khajoori, Block : Nawabganj, Disrict : Unnao

Information displayed on a board as a sign of transparency
Vill : Badi, Block : Sidhauli, District : Sitapur

Digging of a pond : Work in progress

Vill. : Kumhravan, Block : Shivgarh, District : Raebareli

6
Major Findings and Suggestions

Poverty and unemployment were the major issues and concerns of development policy in India since Independence. Although there were significant improvements in poverty reduction over the fast five decades or so, persistence of chronic poverty and lack of employment of opportunities among Indian masses remain major issues to be addressed. In this context, The National Rural Employment Guarantee Act, 2005 was passed by the Parliament and notified on September 07, 2005 for securing the livelihood of the people in the rural areas by guaranteeing 100 days of employment to do unskilled manual job in a financial year to a rural household.

The principal thrust of the present study is to understand the salient features and implementation mechanism of the National Rural Employment Guarantee Scheme (NREGA), issues involved in the implementation stage at the village level and people's perception about the Scheme. The study also tries to provide grassroots realities in implementation process for better understanding and better implementation.

This chapter gives summary conclusion and some concrete suggestions in order to understand the implementation process, people perception and progress of the NREGA Scheme. It is earnestly hoped that if these suggestions are implemented it will make these programmes serve their avowed goal of uplifting the socially and economically deprived population in the real sense. The suggestions are made here on the basis of the field survey in the selected sixteen villages. They reflect the objective appraisal that the research team undertook of the various rural development programmes implemented in the state of Uttar Pradesh with special reference to NREGS.

In chapter one, we have briefly traced poverty alleviation programmes launched by Central and State Governments. Their impact on employment creation and poverty reduction have also been examined. The rationale of the study the rationale for the recent Employment Guarantee Act (NREGA, 2005) and need of present study to examine the implementation of NREGA. The rationale has been drawn by examining poverty alleviation programmes launched by the Central and the State Governments during last fifty years or so. Their impact on employment creation and poverty reduction have also been examined. The rationale of the study, the Maharastra Employment Guarantee Scheme 1977 and the NREGA, 2005 have been briefly described. The research methodology and the objectives of the present study are also part of this chapter.

The second chapter describes the basic objective, salient features and the key implementation mechanism of NREGA. The basic objective of the Act is to enhance livelihood security in rural areas by providing at least 100 days of guaranteed wage employment. This work guarantee can also serve other objectives such as generating productive assets, protecting the environment, empowering rural women, reducing rural-urban migration and fostering social equity.

Chapter three presents the demographic, social

and economic profile of our study area. It includes socio-economic and demographic characteristics of state, districts, villages and households. The socio-economic and demographic profiles indicate that the selected villages have considerable population living below poverty line. Hence, the need and scope NREGS implementation for alleviating the poor from the clutches of poverty. The employment guarantee scheme rightly intends to address the backwardness by generating employment opportunities and thereby removing poverty and social inequality as per policy perception. While our central focus is on the state of U.P., we also try to provide comparative analysis with all-India and also with some major states particularly with the so-called BIMRAU States.

Chapter four contains the NREGS in the Uttar Pradesh. The National Rural Employment Guarantee Act, 2005 (NREGA) has been implemented in the state of Uttar Pradesh as per a notification Rural Development of the State Government – Vide Section 7 of the NREGA No. 107/38-7-2006-8 NERGA dated February 8, 2007 under the Uttar Pradesh Rural Employment Guarantee Scheme (UPREGS). The scheme has been implemented in 22 most backward districts in first phase. These are Azamgarh, Banda, Barabanki, Chandauli, Chitrakoot, Fatehpur, Gorakhpur, Hamirpur, Hardoi, Jalaum, Jaunpur, Kaushambi, Kheri, Kushinagar, Lalitpur, Mahoba, Mirzapur, Pratapgarh, Raebareli, Sitapuri, Sonebhadra and Unnao. These 22 districts constitute about 11% of total 200 identified backward districts all over the country in the first phase of the NREGA implementation. The analysis mainly focuses on the first phase of the NREGS implementation and based on the secondary data available at district level for the period of 2006-07. As per the NREGA guidelines and available data relating to the different aspects of NREGS performance and progress, the analysis broadly focuses on foru major aspects. Such as demand for work and extent to which work have been met; employment generated (in term of person days); number of works completed and creation of community assets; and pattern of fund utilization and wage payments. This analysis focused at state and district level of NREGS first phase implantation.

Chapter five presents the survey results based on the responses from the beneficiaries at the worksites in different villages of selected four districts as per our sample. The survey results show that the majority of beneficiary workers in the age group of 18-35 years old. The majority of workers who sought job under the NREGS in almost all the villages surveyed were from scheduled caste (SCs) and other backward castes. The finding reveals that beneficiaries came from SCs households as casual labour in agriculture and as landless population. Further, the socio-economic profiles of beneficiaries show the objectives and benefits of the NREGA reaching to the target group.

Further, the study team came across various cases as they could interface with the officials, NGOs, and beneficiaries at the time of preliminary visits made to all the four districts and eight selected blocks and sixteen villages in the State. In the light of the experience gained and the benefit of exposure that the research team had, during the last six months, the report attempts to record a few policy suggestions/ agenda for future action.

1. The Chief Development Officer acts as District Programme Coordinator and the Block

Development Officer in every Block acts as the Progamme Officer for the implementation of NREGA in every district.

2. The main work under the scheme is related to water conservation. Digging of tanks is on the top priority in each village Panchayat and a target of two tanks per village has been fixed. However, work related to forestry, brick road building, desilting of canals and Nalas (Drains) is also being taken up. Awareness about the work under the scheme is being created by Gram Sabha, Gram Panchayat, Village level workers and through staging a series of *Nukkad Natak* in some of the villages besides this writing of main features of the scheme has also being found on the walls in some of the villages. Information about the employment to the registered household is given by the Pardhan, village level workers Block Development Officers, etc. orally.
3. There has been no involvement of contractor and the machines also in the works related to scheme.
4. Printed forms and facility of photographs are provided free of costs to the villagers. Village level worker/Gram Vikas Adhikari and Gram Pardhan help in the registration process of the workers.
5. In Barabanki as many as 1054 Panchayat Mitra have already been selected. There would be one Panchayat Mitra in every Gram Panchayat in order to maintain records properly at the Gram Panchayat level and to deposit and relevant data at the respective Block level.
6. Government Panchayat Mitra either to not visit the worksite at all or pay their visits very seldom.

7. There is a vigilance committee in every village and all payments are made before the members of the committee on the Bazar days (Local) on weekly basis. In vigilance and monitoring committee, there are five members from the same village where the work is being undertaken. The committee verifies the work and informs the Gram Panchayat and the B.D.O. / Programme Officer of the Block. The constitution of the committee is as follows :
   - — One member from Scheduled Caste
   - — One member from Backward Caste
   - — One woman member, and
   - — Two other members
8. Although procedure of providing employment to the registered members holding job cards is being followed and records maintained but most of the workers are not adequately aware of the sequence of the process.
9. The disabled and aged person have also being found working under the scheme in Kasim Ganj (Dewa Block) in district Barabanki and in Mehndi Kheda Village, Block Hasan Ganj in district Unnao.
10. It is matter of grave concern that in none of the worksites women members of the registered households where found working in the scheme in all the district. This is probably because of the social inhibition and Parda System. Moreover, the male members of the households do not encourage woman to do arduous manual work.
11. Villagers have felt a great relief in getting the job in their own area and look for increase the job opportunities as well as creation of durable assets

in their villages in order to broaden their resource base.

SUGGESTIONS FOR BETTER IMPLEMENTATION OF THE SCHEME

1. There should be a separate set-up to carry out the work under the NREG scheme at District, Block and Gram Panchayat Levels.
2. The people should be be aware of their entitlements on their own. Therefore, a massive awareness campaign is necessary right from District level to the Gram Sabha level. The quality of the awareness about the scheme is most essential for the success of scheme itself. Since the scheme is demand-driven, so the villagers in need of doing work should make the demand of themselves.
3. The wage rate of the labourers should be revised and increased to the level of "living wage" so that the workers do not feel tempted to leave their village and go to city centres in search of work; at the same time there is need to revise working capacity norms also.
4. There should be a computer and a computer operator along with adequate clerical as well as technical staff at the block level. In other words the block office should be well equipped with logistics support. At the same time there should be uniform formats of data maintenance right from Block level to the District level.
5. The participation of women should be increased by all means in every village.
6. The capability of the Panchayati Raj Institutions, the programme officer and the district, block and

village administrations to formulate the programme, to ensure technical standards in estimates and in execution is limited. It will be essential to enhance their capabilities and provide suitable training and Human Resource Development inputs. If this is not done, there will be deficiencies in the operation of the NREGA.

7. If there is any constraint in providing the guarantee to every adult, the guarantee may appropriately be for the 'family' as unit. Family should be defined to mean husband, wife, children and other dependent members living together.

8. It is necessary to earmark separate funds in the budget awareness creation about the entitlement of the poor for work under NREGA so as to enhance their participation levels in the scheme.

9. Use of ICT intervention must be initiated in the implementation of NREGA everywhere for communication and mobilization, planning, monitoring and grievance redressal system.

The sample size of the study is very small yet it reveals interesting findings. It would be necessary to explore all the aspects of the implementation process and to plug various loopholes.

Annexures

ANNEXURE–1

A. Trends in Poverty and Number of Poor in U.P.

Year	*Unit*	*Uttar Pradesh*		*All India*	
		Population below poverty line	*Increase/ decrease over previous NSS round*	*Population below poverty line*	*Increase/ decrease over previous NSS round*
1	*2*	*3*	*4*	*5*	*6*
1973-74	Lakh no.	535.73	-	3213.36	-
	%	57.07		54.88	
1977-78	Lakh No.	504.37	(-)31.36	3288.95	75.59
	%	49.05	(-)5.9	51.32	2.4
1983	Lakh No.	556.74	52.37	3228.97	(-)59.98
	%	47.07	10.4	44.48	(-)1.8
1987-88	Lakh No.	536.53	(-) 20.21	3070.48	(-)158.49
	%	41.46	(-) 3.6	38.86	(-)4.9
1993-94	Lakh No.	604.45	67.92	3203.68	133.20
	%	40.85	12.7	35.97	4.3
1999-00	Lakh No.	529.89	(-) 74.56	2602.50	(-) 601.18
	%	31.15	(-) 12.3	26.10	(-) 18.77

B. Trends in Unemployment Rate in U.P.

Rounds	*Unemployment rate (15-59)*
27th (1972-73)	3.75
32nd (1977-78)	4.33
38th (1983)	4.71
43rd (1987-88)	3.73
50th (1993-94)	3.46
55th (1999-2000)	4.48

Source: NSS Various Rounds quoted in Human Development Report 2003: Uttar Pradesh

ANNEXURE– 2

SURVEY AREA AND SAMPLE SIZE

S. No.	*Distt.*	*Block*	*Village*	*No. of Beneficiaries interviewed*
1.	Barabanki	Banki	Piparauli	25
			Alapur	25
		Dewa	Kasimganj	25
			Khajurgaon	25
		Total		**100**
2.	Raebareli	Bachharawan	Rasoolpur	25
			Thulendi	25
		Shivagarh	Kumhrawan	25
			Pipari	25
		Total		**100**
3.	Sitapur	Sidhauli	Aladadpur	25
			Badi	25
		Gondalamau	Shamsapur	25
			Kheuta Rampur	25
		Total		**100**
4.	Unnao	Hasanganj	Hasanganj	25
			Mehndi Khera	25
		Nawabganj	Khajoori	25
			Tendua Hiran Kuddi	25
		Total		**100**
		Grant Total		**400**

ANNEXURE – 3
QUESTIONNAIRE

लाल बहादुर शास्त्री रिसर्च सेन्टर फार पब्लिक पालीसी एण्ड सोशल चेन्ज

१, मोती लाल नेहरू प्लेस, नई दिल्ली - ११००११

क्रमांक -.............

राष्ट्रीय ग्रामीण रोजगार गारण्टी योजना

प्रश्नावली

नाम .... *पुत्र/पुत्री/पत्नी* .... *दिनांक* ....

आयु ....*वर्ष* *घर में १८ वर्ष से अधिक सदस्य* .... *ग्राम* ....

जाति - अनुसूचित / पिछड़े / अन्य पिछड़े / सामान्य *ग्राम पंचायत* ....

शिक्षित / अशिक्षित *इण्टरमीडिएट पंचायत* ....

ब्लाक ....*तहसील* ....

जिला ....

प्र01 आपके क्षेत्र में राष्ट्रीय ग्रामीण रोजगार गारण्टी योजना चल रही है, क्या यह आपको मालूम है?
हाँ ☐ नहीं ☐

प्र02 यदि मालूम है, तो आपको कैसे / किससे मालूम हुआ?
रैली से☐ पदयात्रा से ☐ ग्राम सभा से ग्राम पंचायत से ☐
ब्लाक स्तरीय सूचना पट से ☐ ***जिला स्तरीय सूचना पट से***☐

प्र03 आप इसमें रोजगार कर रहे हैं या कर चुके हैं तो क्या आपके पंजीयन के लिए ग्राम सभा ने आपकी मदद की? हाँ ☐ नहीं ☐

प्र04 ग्राम पंचायत में पंजीयन के कितने दिन बाद आपको रोजगार कार्ड (जॉब कार्ड) मिला ?
एक सप्ताह ☐ दो सप्ताह ☐ अधिक समय ☐

प्र05 रोजगार पाने के लिए किसको प्रार्थना पत्र दिया था?
ग्राम पंचायत को ☐ प्रोग्राम आफीसर को ☐ ***प्रधान/उप प्रधान को*** ☐
बीडीसी सदस्य को ☐ ***ग्राम स्तरीय निर्माण एवं कार्यान्वयन समिति को*** ☐
नियोजन समिति को ☐ ***ब्लाक पंचायत विकास अधिकारी को*** ☐

प्र06 क्या आपको प्रार्थना पत्र देने के बाद तारीख पड़ी हुई रसीद दी गई थी?
हाँ ☐ नहीं ☐ याद नहीं ☐

प्र07 क्या आपको रोजगार कार्ड प्राप्त करने के लिए कुछ धन खर्च करना पड़ा? हाँ ☐ नहीं ☐

प्र08 आपको रोजगार मिलने के बारे में कैसे सूचना मिली थी?
ग्राम पंचायत से पत्र द्वारा ☐ प्रोग्राम ऑफीसर से पत्र द्वारा ☐
ग्राम पंचायत कार्यालय के नोटिस बोर्ड से ☐ प्रोग्राम ऑफीसर के नोटिस बोर्ड से ☐
ग्राम स्तरीय समिति के सदस्यों से☐

प्र09 आपने प्रार्थना पत्र में जिस तारीख से काम माँगा था, उसके कितने दिन बाद रोजगार मिला?
एक सप्ताह ☐ दो सप्ताह ☐ अधिक समय ☐

Contd...

प्र010 यदि उस तारीख से 15 दिनों में रोजगार नहीं मिला तो क्या कोई क्षतिपूर्ति या भत्ता मिला?
हाँ ☐ नहीं ☐ अनावश्यक(नॉट एप्लीकेबल) ☐

प्र011 आपको अब तक कितने दिनों का रोजगार मिला है? दिन संख्या ....

प्र012 इस योजना में आपके घर के कितने लोगों ने रोजगार पाया है?
एक ☐ दो ☐ तीन ☐ चार ☐

प्र013 आपकी दैनिक मजदूरी कितनी है? रू0 ....

प्र014 आपको मजदूरी कितने समय में मिलती है / थी ?
एक सप्ताह ☐ दो सप्ताह ☐ अधिक समय ☐

प्र015 क्या आपको बैंक /पोस्ट नेटवर्क से मजदूरी मिलती है / थी ?
बैंक ☐ पोस्ट ☐ नगद ☐

प्र016 क्या मजदूरी पाने में कोई कठिनाई होती है / थी? हाँ ☐ नहीं ☐

प्र017 यदि हाँ तो किस प्रकार की कठिनाई होती है / थी?
1. 2. 3. 4.

प्र018 क्या रोजगार की जगह आपके ग्राग से 5 कि.मी. के अन्दर है/ थी या इससे अधिक दूरी पर है / थी? 5 कि.मी. के अन्दर ☐ 5 कि.मी. से अधिक दूरी पर ☐

प्र०१९ क्या आप पंचायत स्तर पर गठित निगरानी समिति के विषय में जानते हैं? हाँ ☐ नहीं ☐

प्र०२० यदि हाँ तो कौन-कौन इसके सदस्य हैं ?
१. २. ३. ४.

प्र021 क्या मजदूरी का भुगतान बाकी है? हाँ ☐ नहीं ☐

प्र022 क्या काम की जगह पर बच्चों (6 वर्ष से कम) के लिए व्यवस्था है / थी ?
केश की ☐ छाया की ☐ बालवाड़ी की ☐ कुछ नहीं ☐

प्र023 क्या काम की जगह पर व्यवस्था है / थी ?
पीने के पानी की हाँ ☐ नहीं ☐
फर्स्ट एड (तुरन्त उपचार की) हाँ ☐ नहीं ☐

प्र024 रोजगार में किस प्रकार का काम है / था?
1. 2. 3. 4.

प्र025 क्या इस प्रकार के काम होने से ग्रामों में रोजगार के अवसर बढ़ेंगे? हाँ ☐ नहीं ☐

प्र026 क्या आप इस योजना के चलने से प्रसन्न हैं? हाँ ☐ नहीं ☐

प्र027 इस योजना की सफलता के लिए यदि आपके कोई सुझाव हों तो कृपया बताइये–
1. 2. 3. 4.

पर्यवेक्षक की टिप्पणी :--

कार्यस्थल ग्राम

हस्ताक्षर
पर्यवेक्षक (फील्ड इन्वेस्टीगेटर)

ANNEXURE–4

NATIONAL RURAL EMPLOYMENT GUARANTEE SCHEME

Progress Report Date : 8-12-2006

District : Barabanki

1.	Total Fund available	:	Rs.5175.36 Lakhs
2.	Expenditure	:	Rs. 3539.34 Lakhs
3.	No. of application received for registration	:	326521
4.	No. of registered households	:	32314
5.	No. of Job cards distributed	:	326314
6.	No. of Labourers demanding work	:	110510
7.	No. of Mandays for which employment demanded	:	3846320

8. No. of Mandays generated

Total	*Contribution of Schedule Castes*	*Women out of Total*
3685215	2388840	3048

9. No. of Labourers to whom employment provided

Total	*Schedule Castes out of Total*	*Women out of Total*
110510	68841	1442

10.	No. of Households to whom employment provided	:	94119
11.	No. of projects completed	:	934

Source : District Rural Development Agency, Barabanki_ HYPERLINK "http://ruralsoft.up.nic.inis" __http://ruralsoft.up.nic.inis_

ANNEXURE – 5

NATIONAL RURAL EMPLOYMENT GUARANTEE SCHEME

Progress Report — Date : 10-12-2006

Block : Dewa — District-Barabanki

1.	No. of Gram Panchayats	: 76
2.	No. of BPL Households	: 13423
3.	No. of Verified and registered households	: 16845
4.	No. of households eligible for work	: 16945
5.	No. of households demanding work	: 2805
6.	No. of households provided work	: 2795
7.	No. of Total Man days generated	: 34778
	Mandays generated by Schedule Castes	: 24109
	Mandays generated by others	: 10669
	No. of Women in Total	: 12
8.	Funds available on 1.4.2006	: Rs. 7170411 Lakhs
9.	Funds utilized	: Rs.2752560 Lakhs

Source : Development Block Office, Dewa

ANNEXURE – 6

NATIONAL RURAL EMPLOYMENT GUARANTEE SCHEME

Progress Report — Date : 09-12-2006

Block : Banki — District-Barabanki

1.	No. of Gram Panchayats	:	62
2.	No. of BPL Households	:	14718
3.	No. of Verified and registered households	:	16480
4.	No. of Job cards issued	:	16465
5.	No. of Total members of the registered households	:	17117
6.	No. of Households demanded work	:	2258
7.	No. of Members who demanded work	:	2470
8.	No. of Household provided work	:	1718
9.	No. of Mandays for which work was demanded	:	44487
10.	No. of Mandays generated	:	47668
	Mandays generated by Schedule Castes	:	28545
	Mandays generated by others	:	16612
	Contribution of women in total mandays	:	93
11.	No. of Labourers to whom work was provided	:	2452

	No. of Schedule Castes Labourers	:	1709
	No. of Other Labours	:	754
	No. of Women Labourers	:	9
12.	No. of works started in the Block	:	139
13.	Funds available on 1.4.2006	:	Rs.129.397 Lakhs
14.	Fudns utilized w.e.f. 1.4.2006	:	Rs.101.325 Lakhs

Source : Development Block Office, Banki

ANNEXURE – 7
NATIONAL RURAL EMPLOYMENT GUARANTEE SCHEME

Progress Report Date : 07-02-2007

District : Raebareli

1.	No. of Blocks	:	21
2.	No. of applications received for registration	:	366649
3.	No. of registered households	:	342365
4.	No. of job cards distributed	:	326176
5.	No. of applications demanding work	:	185544
6.	No. of Mondays for which demand was made	:	3856265
7.	No. of mandays generated	:	3724431
	No. of mandays contributed by Schedule Castes	:	2086019
	No. of Mandays contributed by Women	:	716118
8.	No. of Labourers provided work	:	170725
	No. of Schedule Castes labourers	:	102435
	No. of Women Labourers	:	51218
9.	No. of households provided work	:	164268
10.	No. of new activities under taken	:	3526

11.	No. of activities already initiated	:	379
12.	No. of activities completed	:	4080
13.	Total Funds available	:	Rs.5276.860 Lakhs
14.	Total Funds utilized	:	Rs.3591.320 Lakhs
	Funds utilized (in percent)	:	68.13

Source : District Rural Development Agency, Raebareli

ANNEXURE – 8
NATIONAL RURAL EMPLOYMENT GUARANTEE SCHEME

Progress Report Date : 22-01-2006

Block : ShivagarhDistrict-Raebareli

1.	No. of Application received for registration	:	13667
2.	No. of Households registered	:	13234
3.	No. of Job cards distributed	:	13234
4.	No. of applications demanding work	:	7354
5.	No. of mandays for which demanded was made	:	134800
6.	No. of Total mandays generated	:	134638
	Contribution of Schedule Castes in mandays generated	:	81200
	Contribution of women in mandays generated	:	2886
7.	No. of labourers provided work	:	7354
	No. of Schedules Castes provided work	:	4578
	No. of women provided work	:	325
8.	No. of Household provided work	:	7118
9.	No. of new activities undertaken	:	371

10.	No. of activities initiated already	:	32
11.	No. of activities completed	:	339
12.	Total Funds available	:	Rs. 168.30 Lakhs
13.	Total Funds utilized	:	Rs.148.16 Lakhs
14.	Total Funds utilized (in percent)	:	88

Source : Development Block Office, Shivagarh.

ANNEXURE – 9

NATIONAL RURAL EMPLOYMENT GUARANTEE SCHEME

Progress Report — Date : 03-02-2007

Block : Bachharawan — District-Raebareli

1.	No. of application received for registration	:	20131
2.	No. of household registered	:	18442
3.	No. of job cards distributed	:	15163
4.	No. of application for demanding work	:	8314
5.	No. of Mandays for which demand was made	:	157968
6.	No. of mandays generated	:	157968
	Contributions of Schedule Castes in Mandays generated	:	94780
	Contribution of women in mandays generated	:	25820
7.	No. of labourers provided work	:	8014
	No. of Schedule Castes Labourers	:	4808
	No. of Women	:	1824
8.	No. of Households provided work	:	7916
9.	No. of activities undertaken	:	108
10.	No. of activities initiated already	:	16

11.	No. of activities completed	:	165
12.	Total funds available	:	Rs.232.765 Lakhs
13.	Total funds utilized	:	Rs.188.540 Lakhs
14.	Total Funds utilized (in percent)	:	81

Source : Development Block Office, Bachharawan

ANNEXURE – 10

NATIONAL RURAL EMPLOYMENT GUARANTEE SCHEME

Progress Report Date : 12-02-2007

District-Sitapur

1.	No. of Blocks	: 19
2.	No. of Job cards distributed	: 313712
3.	No. of Mandays to be generated	: 4385168
4.	No. of mandays actually generated	: 3990360
	Contribution of Schedule Castes in total mandays	: 2585170
	Contribution of women in total mandays	: 20363
5.	Total no. of laboures provided work	: 206697
	No. of Schedule Castes labourers	: 144598
	No. of women labourers	: 2272
6.	Total funds available	: Rs.6931.751 Lakhs
7.	Total funds utilized	: Rs.4501.849 Lakhs
	Total funds utilized (in percent)	: 64.95

Source : District Rural Development Agency, Sitapur

ANNEXURE – 11

NATIONAL RURAL EMPLOYMENT GUARANTEE SCHEME

Progress Report — Year : 2005-06

Block : Sidhauli — District-Sitapur

1.	No. of Gram Panchayats	:	71
2.	No. of applications received for registration	:	11107
3.	No. of job cards distributed	:	10620
	To Schedule Castes	:	6961
	To others	:	3659
4.	No. of households demanded work	:	4760
	No. of Labourers demanded work	:	5758
5.	No. of Households provided work	:	4556
	No. of labourers provided work	:	6469

Source : Development Block Office, Sidhauli

ANNEXURE – 12

NATIONAL RURAL EMPLOYMENT GUARANTEE SCHEME

Progress Report — Date : 15.12.06

Block : Gondalamau — District-Sitapur

1.	No. of applications received for registration	:	16798
2.	No. of job cards distributed	:	14978
	To Schedule Castes	:	10213
	To others	:	4765
3.	No. of Households demanded work	:	5272
	No. of labourers demanded work	:	7781
4.	No. of households provided work	:	5241
	No. of Labourers provided	:	10188
	No. of Schedule Castes workers	:	5984
5.	No. of women workers	:	130

Source : Development Block Office, Gondalamau

ANNEXURE – 13

NATIONAL RURAL EMPLOYMENT GUARANTEE SCHEME

Progress Report Date : 30.01.2007

District-Unnao

1.	No. of Blocks	:	16
2.	No. of BPL households	:	283194
3.	No. of applications received for registration	:	205332
4.	No. of job cards distributed	:	203041
5.	No. of applications received for demanding work	:	112691
6.	No. of labourers provided work	:	112691
	No. of Schedule Castes workers provided work	:	67901
7.	No. of households which were provided work for 100 days	:	298

Source : District Rural Development Agency, Unnao

ANNEXURE – 14

NATIONAL RURAL EMPLOYMENT GUARANTEE SCHEME

Progress Report — Date : 7-2-2007

Block : Nawabganj — District-Unnao

1.	No. of Gram Panchayats	:	72
2.	No. of job cards distributed	:	13532
3.	No. of registerd households	:	14327
4.	No. of mandays generated	:	2.21 Lakhs

Source : Development Block Office, Nawabganj

ANNEXURE – 15

NATIONAL RURAL EMPLOYMENT GUARANTEE SCHEME

Progress Report Date : 18-2-2007

Block : Hasanganj District-Unnao

1.	No. of Gram Panchayats	: 70
2.	No. of applications received for registration	: 9397
3.	No. of registered households after verification	: 9551
4.	No. of job cards distributed	: 9260
5.	No. of application for demand of work	: 4693
6.	No. of workers provided work	: 4693
7.	No. of mandays generated	: 162606
8.	Funds available	: Rs.275.357 Lakhs
9.	Funds utilized	: Rs.149.45156 Lakhs
10.	Funds utilized (in percent)	: 78

Source : Development Block Office, Hasanganj

Select Bibliography

Acharya, Shankar (2004), "Guaranteeing jobs or fiscal crisis", Business Standard, 30 November.

Agarwal, S. and Saha, R. (2004), "Give it more teeth", Financial Express, 25 December.

Aiyar, Swaminathan S. Anklesaria (2004), Poverty Reduction by Helicopter, Times of India, 19 December.

Alexander, P.C. (2004), "Guaranteeing employment", The Asian Age, December.

Banerji, A., and Bardhan, P. (2004), "Food for Thought", Hindustan Times, 15 December.

Basu, Arnab K, Nancy H. Chau and Ravi Kanbur (2005): "The National Rural Employment Guarantee Act of India, 2005", processed, Department of Applied Economics and Management, Cornell University, Ithaca, NY.

Bhaduri, Amit (2004), "Guaranteeing employment", The Hindu, 27 December.

Bidwai, Praful (2004), "UPA Betrays Its Biggest Promise, Mocking at Job Guarantee", The News International, 23 December.

Bisht, Arvind Singh. 2006. 'Rural employment: No guarantee yet', *The Times of India*, New Delhi, 19 February, viewed 13th October 2006.

Chakravarti, Sauvik 2006. 'Employment Guarantee a Hoax', Indian *Express*, New Delhi, 6 August, viewed 15th October 2006.

Chamaraj, Kathyayini (2004), "People as Puppets", The Hindu, 8 August.

Chandra Mohan, N. 2005. 'Jobbing through to the elections', *Sify.com*, 5 October, viewed 15th October

Chandrasekhar and Jayati Ghosh (2004), "How feasible is a rural employment guarantee", Hindu Business Line, 22 June.

Chary, V.R. 2005. 'Regs: Grossly Miscalculated?', *The Hindu Business Line*, 7 September, viewed 15th October 2006

Chatterjee, Manini. 2005. 'Spoils of the soil' *Indian Express*, New Delhi, 16 October,

Dev, S. Mahendra (2004), "Employment Guarantee Scheme at the National Level", Economic Times, December.

Dogra, Bharat. 2005. 'Jobs and options', *The Times of India*, New Delhi, viewed 15th

Drèze, Jean (2004), "Unemployment Guarantee Bill", The Hindu, 31 December.

Drèze, Jean (2004), "Why should anyone be afraid of the Employment Guarantee Act?", Financial Express, 17 December.

Drèze, Jean (2004), Employment as a social responsibility, The Hindu, 22 November.

Dreze, Jean. 2006. 'National employment guarantee inaction', *The Hindu*, Chennai, 12 September, viewed 13th October 2006.

Gaiha, Raghav (2004), "No 100 per cent guarantee", Indian Express, 20 December.

Ghosh, Avijit, 2006. 'Job scheme gets feminised in south Rajasthan', *The Times of India*, New Delhi, 26 April, viewed 13th October 2006.

Ghosh, Jayati (2004), "Rural Employment as a policy priority", Frontline, 3 July.

Ghosh, Jayati, How to pay for the Employment Guarantee (Macroscan, December 2004)

Gokarn, Subir, Employer of the Last Resort, Business Standard, 20 December.

Grinspun, Alejandro. 2005. 'Three models of social protection', International Poverty

Gupta, Smita (2004), "Promises to Keep", Frontline, 18 December.

Gupta, Smita, Employment Guarantee: An Act to Salvage Democracy (Macroscan, December 2004)

Hasan, Zoya (2005), "EGA: Needed, a govt guarantee Act", Indian Express, 6 January.

Iqbal, Mohammad. 2006. 'Public vigilance helps to minimise corruption in rural

Jain, L.C. (2004), "Work is the crux, so is self-governance", Financial Express, 17 December.

Jain, Sachin Kumar. 2006. 'Digging in times of harvest', *Tehelka*, New Delhi, 1 July,

Jain, Sonu. 2005. 'Rich, poor, all states are in job guarantee net', *The Indian Express*, New Delhi, 8 December, viewed 13th October 2006.

Jain, Sonu. 2006. 'Job Guarantee rolls out, ray of hope in New Delhi shadow', *The Indian*

Jain, Sunil (2004), "Making an ass of u and me", Business Standard, 25 October.

Karat, Brinda (2004), "No jobs ahead: Dilutions in Employment law unacceptable", Times of India, December 11.

Khera, Reetika. 2006. 'Employment Guarantee and Migration', *The Hindu*, Chennai, 13 July, viewed 13th October 2006.

Lakshman, Nirmala. 2006. 'Employment guarantee — signs of transformation', The Hindu, Thursday, May 11

McGivering, Jill. 2006. 'Is India's rural poverty plan working?', BBC News, 22 April, viewed 13th October 2006.

Mehrotra, Santosh (2004), "Can India really do without EGS?", Economic Times, 20 December.

Menon, Sreelatha. 2006. 'Fake entry is the buzzword at Dungarpur work sites', *Business Standard*, New Delhi, 7 August.

Menon, Sreelatha. 2006. 'Here the policy is to discourage women', *Business Standard*, New Delhi, 11 August.

Menon, Sreelatha. 2006. 'Rajasthan tops states in job card holders', *Business Standard*, New Delhi, 10 August.

Menon, Sreelatha. 2006. 'Why low wages do not pass muster here?' *Business Standard*, New Delhi, 9 August.

Mohan, N. Chandra (2004), "Guaranteeing work in India's countryside" Financial Express, 23 December.

Morris, Sebastian. 2005. 'Employment Guarantee Scheme is a still-born child: Try land Reforms', *Financial Express*, August 30, viewed 15th October 2006

Narayan, S., Convenience of Employment Guarantees, The Financial Express, 8 December.

Nayak, Pulin B., Building Blocks, *The Hindustan Times*, New Delhi, May 31, 2007

Ninan, T.N., Guaranteeing Work, Business Standard, 18 December. October 2006

Olson, Maxine, 2005. 'Work for pro-poor growth', *The Economic Times*, New Delhi, 20 October, viewed 13th October 2006.

Patnaik, Ila (2004), "Sincere about job guarantee? Give up subsidies you milk", Indian Express, 9 December.

Patnaik, Prabhat (2005), "Need for a universal EGS", The Hindu, 5 January.

Raja, D., Employment is a Right (The Financial Express, November 24, 2004)

Ramanathan, Ramesh (2004), "Time to reflect on rural jobs bill?", Financial Express, 17 December.

Rao, Bhanoji, NREG Bill: Fine Tuning Will Make it Work Better, Business Line, 4 January.

Rao, Jaithirth (2004), "Forget efficiency. Let's do it", Indian Express, 10 December.

Reddy, C. Rammanohar and Vijayshankar, P. (2004), "Making Employment Guarantee"

Reality", Seminar, Number 541, September.Debroy, Bibek (2004), "Jobs, not the government's job", Indian Express, 13 October.

Roy, Aruan and Khera, Reetika (2005), "Not everybody loves a good drought", The Hindu Magazine, 2 January.

Roy, Bunker (2005), "100 days that will change India", Indian Express, 5 January.

Shah, Mihir (2004), "A workable right to employment", The Hindu, 24 August.

Shah, Mihir (2005), "Saving the NREGA", The Hindu, January.

Shah, Mihir. 2004. 'National Rural Employment Guarantee Act: A Historic Opportunity', Economic Political Weekly, Decembe· 11, 2004.

Shah, Rajiv. 2006. 'Report slams state record on rural jobs', *The Times of I ndia*, Gandhi Nagar, 15 September, viewed 13th October 2006.

Sharma, Sandipan. 2006. 'Centre planning EGA wage cut, say activists on ground', *TheIndian Express*, New Delhi, 28 April, viewed 13th October 2006.

Shiva Kumar, A.K. 2005. 'Purposeful employment creation', *Education World Online*, October 2006

Singh, Tavleen. 2005. 'Marxists begin to see the light Not Sonia', *Indian Express*, Sunday August 28, viewed 15th October 2006.

Singhvi, Abhishek (2004), "Just the Job", Hindustan Times, 15 December.

Sood, Tanushree. 2006. 'NREGA: Challenges in implementation', *InfoChange News &Features*, September, viewed 13th October 2006. http://www.infochangeindia.org/features380.jsp

Sridhar, V. 2005. 'Empowering the rural poor', Frontline, Volume 22 - Issue 19, Sep 10 -23, 2006.

Srinivasan, T.N. (2005), "Guaranteeing Employment: A Palliative?", The Hindu, 3 January.

Status of NREGA Implementatioatus of NREGA Implementation.

Times News Network, 'UP a laggard in the rural job plan', *The Times of India*, New Delhi, 9 August, viewed 13th October 2006.

Vaidyanathan, A. 2005. 'Employment Guarantee and Decentralization', Economic and Political Weekly, April 16.

Venkitaramanan, S., Job Schemes Must Effect Grassroots Changes, Business Line, 13 December. 2006.

INDEX